W9-AVO-249

REVIEW IS INSIDE LAST PAGE

STAINED GLASS
WORKSHOP

Dedicated once more to Roberto and our little daughter.

Acknowledgements
To all those who helped me in successfully completing this manual:
To FANTASY CRAFT, Milan, via Desiderio 3/9 (www.fantasycraft.it) for supplying me with all of the necessary materials, tools, and glass photographed in the text, as well as with the Dover books from which some examples were taken.
To Annarita Aloni, my long-time, irreplaceable collaborator.
To Marina Passarella, who made some of the photographed panels.
To Dott. Conti of APA, who supplied the Ferrario colors used for the mock stained glass panels.
Special thanks are due to Alberto Bertoldi for his skill in photographing the work.

Those who wish to know more about the techniques and to learn new ones, may request the program and dates of the courses held by the author at FANTASY CRAFT, via Desiderio 3/9, Milan. Tel: 02/7063 4689; e-mail: fantasycraft@tiscalinet.it

Editor: Cristina Sperandeo
Photography: Alberto Bertoldi
Translation: Chiara Tarsia
Graphic design and layout: Paola Masera and Amelia Verga

Library of Congress Cataloging-in-Publication Data Available

1 0   9   8   7   6   5   4   3   2   1

Published by Sterling Publishing Company, Inc.
387 Park Avenue South, New York, NY 10016
First published in Italy by RCS Libri S.p.A.
under the title *La vetrata artistica e le sue tecniche*
© 1999 RCS Libri S.p.A., Milan 1st Edition Great Fabbri Manuals September 1999
© 2001 English translation by Sterling Publishing Co., Inc.
Distributed in Canada by Sterling Publishing Co., Inc.
C/o Canadian Manda Group, One Atlantic Avenue, Suite 105
Toronto, Ontario, Canada M6K 3E7
Distributed in Great Britain and Europe by Cassell PLC
Wellington House, 125 Strand, London WC2R 0BB, England
Distributed in Australia by Capricorn Link (Australia) Pty Ltd.
P.O. Box 704, Windsor, NSW 2756, Australia

Sterling ISBN 0-8069-7607-1

Maria di Spirito

STAINED GLASS WORKSHOP

Sterling Publishing Co., Inc.
New York

CONTENTS

INTRODUCTION

The techniques of working and decorating glass were once only known to a small number of experts, who handed down their knowledge from generation to generation, and imparted practical skill through long apprenticeships. Today, thanks to the vast number of specific books on the subject and to the availability of tools, anyone in possession of patience, precision, and some spark of creativity may try his or her hand at this most satisfying artistic activity. We can create attractive glass panels for our own use, or for friends, where a personal touch makes it even more precious. The aim of this manual is to explain to those, who are approaching this fascinating world for the first time, the basic working techniques of artistic glasswork and to describe the various technical steps in a simple manner. The techniques we used in this manual are: Tiffany, traditional, collage, mock, etched, and grisaille. For each technique, we have prepared a panel of average difficulty and described the various steps. Furthermore, colored photographs of completed projects are included to encourage your personal creativity. A section of the book has even been dedicated to the different types of glass available on the market to help you get started right away!

Maria di Spirito

CLASSICAL
STAINED GLASS

TIFFANY STAINED GLASS

This technique received its name from its creator, Louis Comfort Tiffany. Thanks to him, the art of stained glass enjoyed a period of great splendor around the turn of the last century, totally changing the taste of the times. The secret of his success lay in his tenacity and perfectionism, but above all else, stemmed from his endless search for a production that would mirror the changes in style dictated by the prevailing fashions. Tiffany began his career by opening a glasswork capable of creating glass with the features, which he himself was looking for, and which were not available in the market. What then was the innovative characteristic of his glass as compared to that of other manufacturers? With his technique, the colors were present within the sheet of glass itself. Therefore, there was no need for further pictorial embellishment with surface decorations. Tiffany's other great innovation was his technique for assembling the panel. The glass pieces were first edged with thin strips of copper (copper foil), then positioned on the pattern and soldered together. Prior to Tiffany, lead came was used for the grooves where the glass was inserted. Compared to lead came, copper foil is much easier to use and more practical, which makes it possible to create glass shapes in virtually any size or detail.

A simple panel greatly appreciated for its elegance. The background glass is gray cathedral. The frames are fractures of transparent glass with chips in pink, green, and light blue. The roses are made from fine, deep pink colorescent glass, while the leaves are green ring mottled opalescent.

TRADITIONAL STAINED GLASS

During the medieval period, plaster, stucco, and wooden frames were used as the supporting materials for stained glass. The later employment of lead came made it possible to reduce the width of the mountings and consequently to lighten the weight of the structures. In Europe, mostly in Italy where the religious cult was widespread, traditional leaded stained glass depicted sacred images. It certainly still is today the most widely used for both sacred and profane decorations. This technique permits savings in time and costs, as the panels can only be simple and linear due to construction requirements. Lead came, which is relatively flexible, may only be used to frame glass of simple cuts, and of medium or large dimensions. This technique is considered the most economic and is known and used by almost all glass workers. Surface coloring with enamel or grisaille may be used as decorative elements to a panel, which would otherwise seem too elementary. The traditional stained glass technique is suitable for creating all types of projects, whether of small, medium, or large dimensions. It also is the best for constructing panels, which require a rigid structure. It is advisable, however, not to exceed one square yard, and, where a larger size is required, to contact an expert for help in making a suitable frame capable of containing several panels. The end result will appear as one single panel. In fact, the great storied windows in cathedrals are comprised of hundreds of small panels, which were then laid out and secured to one single, enormous frame.

The center of the medallion is in transparent cathedral glass with decorations in grisaille and color, while the remainder is blown colored glass.

COLLAGE STAINED GLASS

Collage is the most modern or innovative technique used for making stained glass. Up until the stage of cutting the glass, the various working phases are the same as the traditional and Tiffany techniques. Instead of being assembled with lead came or copper foil, the glass pieces are covered with Resin-glass and then placed on a frame of prepared transparent glass. The main artistic feature of collage glass is the absence of the highlighted outlines of the design. The result is a very light and transparent composition. Resin-glass, which encases the individual pieces of glass and secures them to the frame, makes the panel very resistant and therefore suitable for creating tables or decorating various types doors.

Collage glass can also be used outdoors, in the bathroom, or for the shower walls. Panels created with other techniques would be damaged by dampness, and the soldering would oxidize. Another very important feature of this technique is that large sized panels can easily be created. Although little known at the moment, there is no doubt that it will very soon find its place in all sectors concerning stained glass; thanks to its resistance, airy composition, and complete absence of size limits.

A window inspired by Mondrian.
Multicolored cathedral glass and
Resin-glass were used to give this window
a vibrant effect, which symbolizes water.

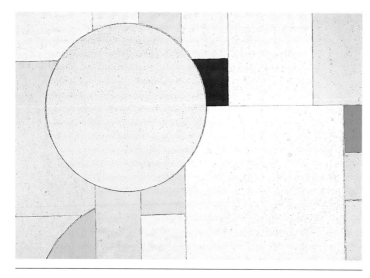

MOCK STAINED GLASS

Mock stained glass was created for decorating rapidly, cheaply, and without any knowledge of glass cutting techniques. Even those without any special manual skill or artistic talent can venture a try at this eye-catching work with this technique, which exactly reproduces leaded glasswork. Both traditional stained glass, made up of glass panels joined by lead came, and Tiffany glasswork, joined with copper foil, may be simulated in this way. Only an expert in this field could tell that the glass was not cut and leaded, and that the decoration is carried out on the panel surface with adhesive lead came and colors. With this technique it is possible to make partitioning doors, furniture panels, screens, pictures, and mirrors. Even glass craftsmen are beginning to appreciate and use this technique, which they find suitable for those clients who wish to renovate the interior of their homes with a work of glass art, but are not willing to take on heavy costs. Even though it makes eye-catching effects possible, this technique is fairly easy to use. However, it must be kept in mind that success does not only depend on a happy choice of subject, but also on the type and color of the background glass, as well as on the proper application of the lead came and colors.

This panel shows how a very complex design may be created with a fairly simple technique. For the background, aquamarine cathedral glass was used. The lead came was treated with a black patina to highlight the design even more.

ETCHED STAINED GLASS

During the last few years there has been a rediscovery of this glass technique, so simple yet so elegant and evocative. It has acquired new value as a valid alternative to traditional stained glass techniques, both on the part of glass lovers and of glass craftsmen themselves. This technique consists in corroding the surface of a given area (corresponding to the design), which creates a white opaque, satin-like look to the treated part. Motifs cut on the glass are permanent. The underlying principle of etching is quite simple. The glass parts, which are not etched, are masked with transparent adhesive plastic. The pattern will stand out due to the contrast between the treated and the transparent parts. All types of glass may be treated with the etching technique: transparent, blown, cathedral, opalescent, etc. This technique is great for: windows, screen panels, furniture, dividing doors, mirrors, and pictures. Your idea is only limited by soldering seams or by the size of the panels. Very detailed patterns may be designed and then carried out with the utmost speed, and not to mention, low costs. The sanding technique partially uses the same procedure. In this case, however, as rather complex instruments are required to finish off the work, it is necessary to use the services of a specialized workshop.

Though this pattern seems simple and unobtrusive, it is difficult to carry out. In order to make the glass more transparent and to let whatever is placed behind it be seen, the decorative motif must be etched instead of the background, as shown here in our example.

STAINED GLASS WITH GRISAILLE

In past times, stained glass panels were not made exclusively with leaded colored glass. They were also enriched with painted decorations, which highlighted the details of the composition as well. The procedure for painting with grisaille, used for centuries, has remained practically unchanged. The technique suggested in the following pages differs in no way from the traditional one. In its oldest form, the technique with grisaille was monochromatic, as the decoration consisted merely in design and shading, while color came from the glass itself. The grisaille was just spread on the glass and then removed, leaving uncovered areas, which allowed light to filter through and create the evocative shadings that are so much a feature of traditional stained glass. Working with grisaille is complex and exacting. First of all, the templates must be made and the glass cut, as for any type of panel. Then the pieces must be decorated and baked in the oven before being assembled with copper foil or lead came. With this technique, decorative panels or panes for interior decorating can be made from any type of glass. The catch is that the pieces must be baked. Those who do not have a furnace may apply to an art school or a craft center for this phase of the work.

This oval panel in blown leaded glass reproduces the motif of "Flower", a work by Alphonse Muchà dating from 1897. The leaded seams coincide with the significant lines of the drawing so as not to spoil the structure of the original design. Dark brown grisaille is used for the edging and old brown for the shading, while just a few colors are used to create the floral composition.

GLASS:
THE BASIC ELEMENT

A SHORT HISTORICAL OUTLINE

Glass was discovered during the Bronze Age, around 5,000 BC, and probably happened by chance. It seems that the Phoenicians found traces of vitreous material, which had formed near fires they had lit on the beach. It was widely used in the east by the Egyptians and Sumerians. The Romans particularly used it for blown glass containers. The first findings, which go back to 100 BC, were: glass goblets, vases, and drinking glasses that were for domestic use.

The first recorded production of flat glass in sheets dates from the 1st century AD. The Romans used it for window vanes, but the cost was high and use was therefore mostly restricted to public buildings. It was not until early medieval times that sheets of glass were assembled with lead came, thus creating the first artistic glass panels. These were then placed in the cathedrals.

The earliest "industrial" glassworks, which supplied the "studios", specialized in making stained glass for the churches. They were usually set up outside the city, almost always near forests in order to obtain the wood necessary for supplying the heat to the ovens. The glassworks at Torcello and Altare were already in operation during medieval times, as were other minor ones in northern Italy. The earliest and most detailed essay about glass was from a man named Theophilus. He probably was a monk who wrote it at the beginning of the 12th century AD in a northern German monastery. Theophilus, who presents himself as an expert in this field, attempts, in the second of three books, to explain the techniques for making stained glass panels.

He also wrote about the processes in glass making, from furnace construction to blowing techniques. During the Middle Ages glass was made from vegetable ashes, mostly derived from ferns. Their function was to lower the fusion point of the silica based river sand, the second component of the mixture. Besides originating from the combustion of ferns, the ashes could also come from beech leaves or seaweed. This mixture was placed in furnaces from 2,000°F up to a maximum of 2,700°F, depending on the quantity of flux (soda or potash) in the vegetation ashes. High percentages of soda and potash resulted in the easy corrosion of the glass. The molten glassy mass was poured onto a stone surface and then, with the help of pliers, lengthened and widened. Only later was blowing used to produce flat glass. Huge balls of

glass were obtained which, pieced at the base, were whirled until they widened into large circular disks.

CHEMISTRY AND PHYSICS

Glass is found in nature as sand, quartz, and siliceous rocks. In physics, glass is a highly viscous liquid, which appears to have the features of a solid. The explanation of the non-formation of the crystal structure lies in the anomalous arrangement, which the components take on during the solidification and cooling phases. From the chemical point of view, glass can be defined as anhydride siliceous or silica (an atom of silica and two of oxygen). Industrial glass is mostly made up of siliceous sand mixed with flux (calcium carbonate or soda sulfate), whose function is to lower the fusion point of the main element at 2,400°F - 2,700°F. Other elements, such as thermal and mechanical stabilizers, are added to the basic composition to obtain mass and color homogeneity and to facilitate the working and shaping of the glass. To color and make the glass opaque, various metallic oxides are added when mixing the powders, such as: copper, iron, cobalt, manganese, tin, or titanium oxides. The successful

mixture of colors reveals the experience and skill of the maker. The mixture making up the glass is then melted in the furnace. The elements amalgamate and the gases contained in the mass can evaporate. The vitreous mass is then left to acquire consistency and transparency, which takes place at about 1,500°F. At this point, work on the glass can begin (blowing, molding, or rolling). Re-baking and long cooling help to make the glass more resistant for subsequent working processes and use.

TYPES AND CHARACTERISTICS

Glass production today offers a huge variety of transparent and colored glass, made both by craftsmen and industries. Experimental processes are continuously adding different varieties to the market. In view of the wide range of possibilities, choosing and buying glass are perhaps the most important moments in the process of constructing a panel. Comparing the various characteristics and imagining the glass in its finished form is exciting and satisfying. The following pages contain examples of the most common types of glass along with their main characteristics.

IRIDESCENT GLASS

All types of art glass, whether transparent or opalescent, may be subjected to processes, which result in a mother-of-pearl effect. This is achieved by vaporizing the metal salts on the surface at a certain heat. When lit from the rear, iridescent glass shimmers with color and looks like normal art glass. When lit from another angle, it has a mother-of-pearl effect.

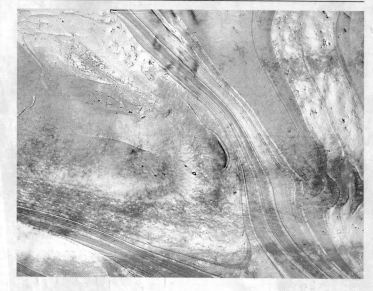

BAROQUE GLASS

This is a rather precious glass with an evenly colored surface presenting large waves, which give clear chiaroscuro effects caused by the varying concentration of the vitreous mass. This glass is generally used for highly effective backgrounds and creates a dramatic result.

WATER GLASS

This glass has an even, wavy surface. The coloring is uniform and monochromatic with beautiful warm tones. The particular structure of this glass gives the stimulating presence of water. It is particularly suitable for backdrops and panels of geometric designs.

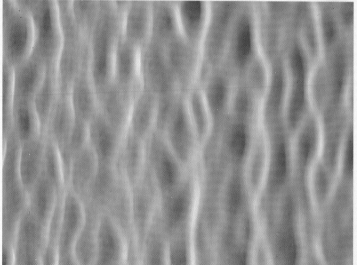

OPALESCENT GLASS

This glass is mostly used for panels. Its name tells us its main characteristic, a milky, semi-translucent look. Solid color opals are available, but generally the color is not uniform, which gives the glass a marbled effect. The coloring of this glass may be monochrome or the same sheet may have various color combinations.

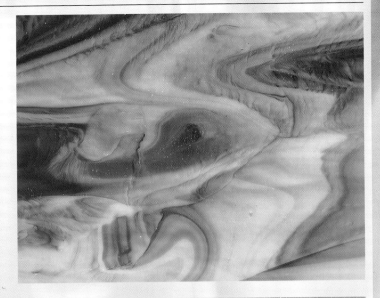

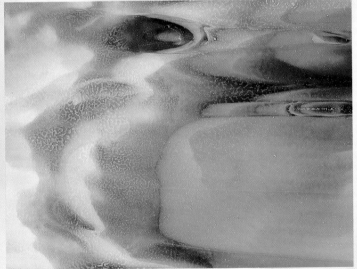

RING MOTTLED GLASS

This glass made Louis Comfort Tiffany famous. Still produced today, it counts as one of the most spectacular and prestigious glasses used for panels. The beauty and brilliancy of its color show up whether lit from behind or from another angle. This glass, more than others, changes its effects when light shines on it. Just a tiny bit of light is all that is needed to make the rings widen and intensify, glowing brightly. The play of light can therefore greatly modify the color and the effect.

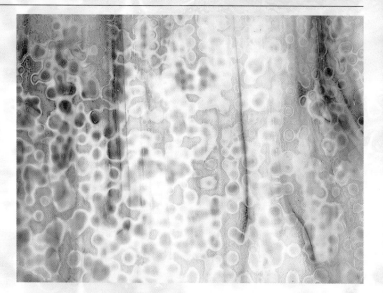

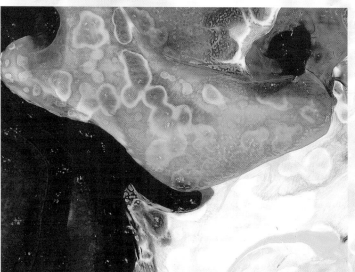

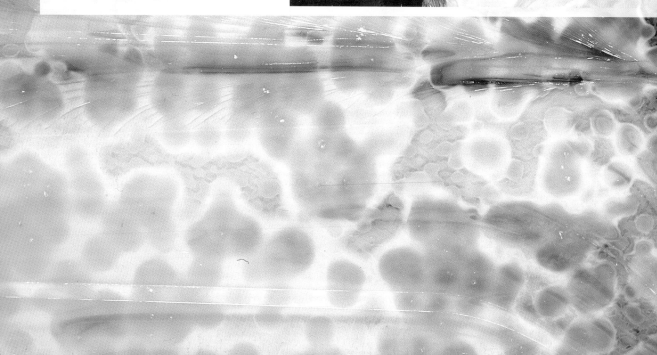

COLORESCENT GLASS

This glass has the typical marble look of opalescent glass, though its background is not opal-white but transparent.
The variety of this glass is surprising: tone-on-tone of the same color, various matching colors, semi-translucent (which allow light to filter through), and others deeply colored.

FRACTURES

This glass, which may have a background structure of transparent or opalescent glass, is characterized by the inclusion of thin chips of colored glass on the surface. It too was invented by the Tiffany Studios and is still made today by hand using the same technology.

GRANITE LIKE GLASS

This type of glass, traditionally handmade, gives the best results in rendering plastic or sculptured effects. Its main feature is an irregular grain, which appears very much like the rough surface of stone. It is sometimes monochrome but usually sports at least three or four attractively mixed colors.

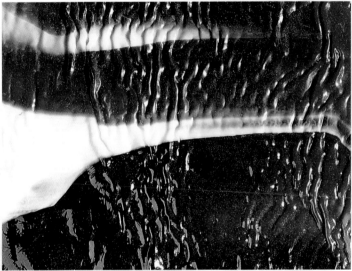

HOW TO CHOOSE GLASS

After the sketch has been prepared, the glass must be chosen. Of course to do this the needs of the composition and personal taste take over, but one must also bear a few simple rules in mind:

— The lighting conditions must be considered since the beauty of stained glass heavily relies on the different effects that it creates.

— Glass that is transparent or clear-colored lets the light filter through, in contrast to dark and opal glass that mask it.

— It is better to choose and check the combination of various pieces of glass with different reflected lights in order to estimate their mutual interference.

— For panel backgrounds use transparent colored glass, as it highlights the composition and gives a sense of depth. Visually speaking, it tends to recede with respect to more compact glass.

— For composition details, choose opal glass because it absorbs the light. If this principle is not followed, the composition will turn out flat and loose that perspective contrast which must exist between the background and the subject.

— Do not use more than four or five types of glass per composition, but use instead the chromatic differences present in the same sheet of glass.

— White, amber, green, and all very light colors, in general, are fairly easy to cut. Deep reds, pinks, and yellows are hard to cut and are fragile.

— Sometimes irregularities are found on the surface of the glass. These, as well as any color differences or marks, are not to be taken as defects but as proof that craftsmen did the work. For this reason it is almost impossible to find two sheets alike.

— Always purchase sufficient supplies of glass to see you through to the end, as it might be impossible to get the same type of glass later.

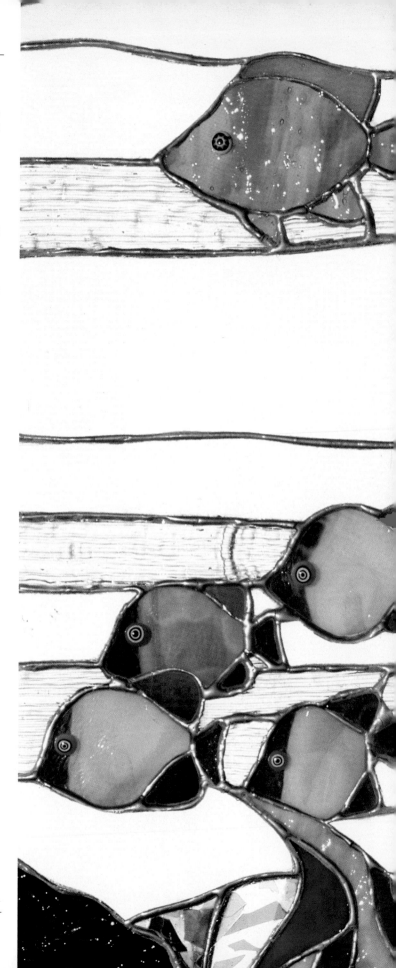

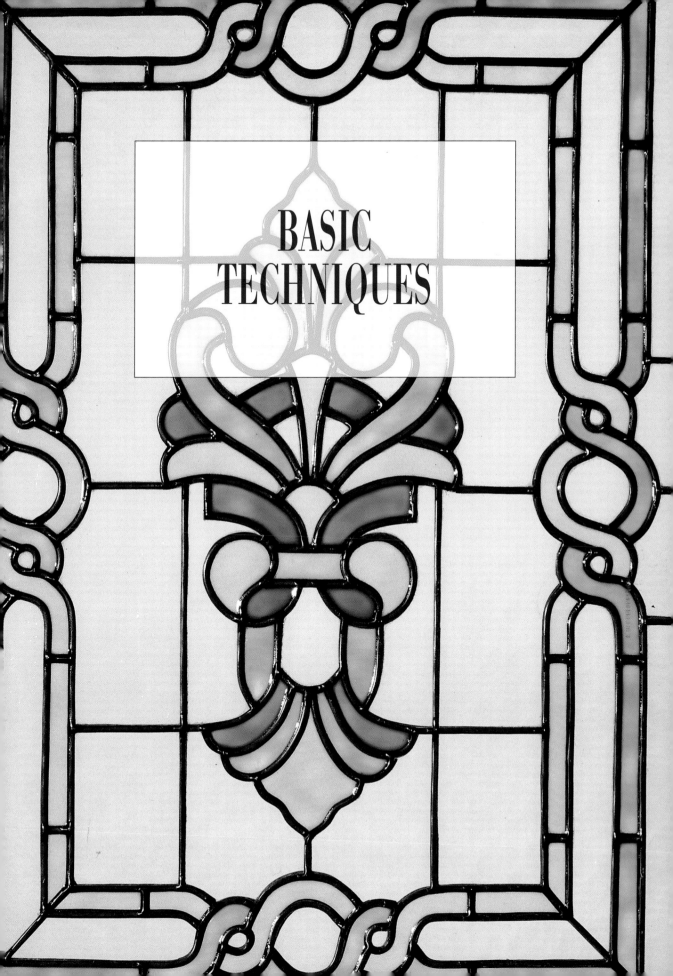

BASIC TECHNIQUES

MATERIALS FOR DRAWING THE PATTERN

Every project presented in this manual is preceded by a preparatory phase during which the patterns and templates are made. Photographed here are the basic tools for drawing, coloring, and cutting. It is good to always have these on hand before starting any project.

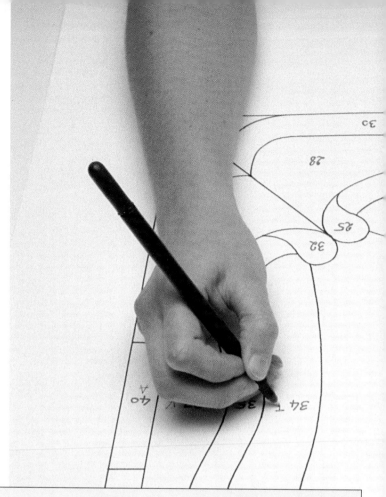

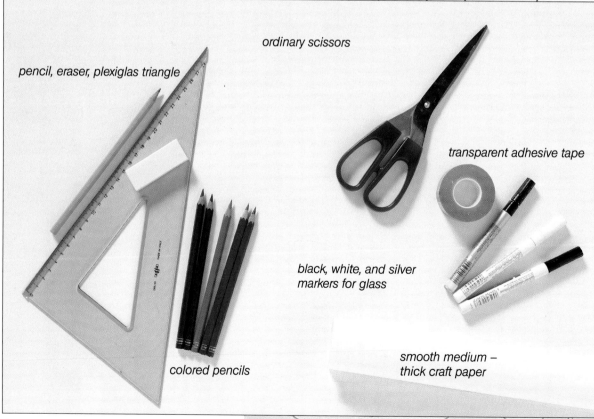

pencil, eraser, plexiglas triangle

ordinary scissors

transparent adhesive tape

colored pencils

black, white, and silver markers for glass

smooth medium – thick craft paper

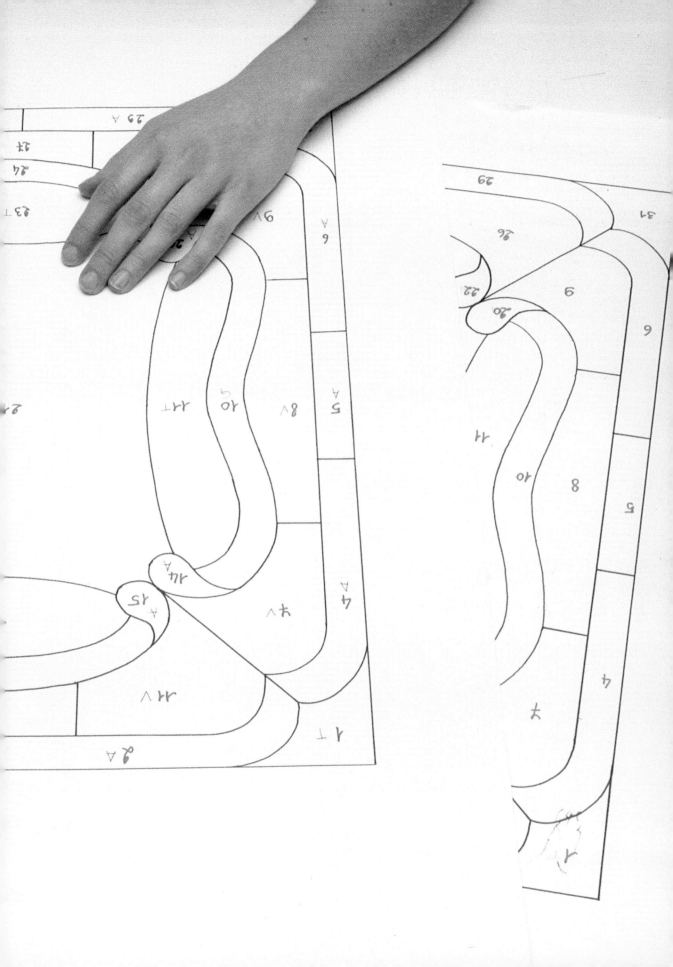

CUTTING AND GRINDING

GLOVES FOR GLASS To be used only for moving and cutting large sheets of glass.

A GRID SURFACE Its honeycomb structure catches glass splinters.

GLASS CUTTING SQUARE Thanks to a clamp, this perpendicularly locks on the side of the glass sheet.

SELF-LUBRICATING GLASS CUTTER This is the most commonly used cutter. It is practical, handy, and has a transparent handle.

MECHANICAL GLASS CUTTER This comes with two regulating knobs, one for pressure and the other for height.

OIL FOR GLASS CUTTERS This is used to constantly keep the wheel lubricated.

PLASTIC RUNNING PLIERS These pliers have a curved lower jaw that is placed directly over the score line and have two marks on the upper jaw.

CURVED RUNNING PLIERS/ BREAKER PLIERS These have a tip on their lower jaw to be positioned at the back of the score line and a movable segment on the upper jaw.

NARROW JAW GROZING PLIERS AND COMBINATION GROZING PLIERS These are used to cut away any remaining fragments. Their jaws measure 1/4" or 1/2" respectively.

MOSAIC GLASS CUTTER These are used like scissors to eliminate excess glass.

SAFETY GLASSES These are used to protect your eyes from dust and splinters.

STEEL WOOL FILE This has an abrasive action.

ELECTRIC GRINDER WITH LUBRICATOR AND SPRAY GUARD The water, which lubricates the rotating bit, keeps glass dust down.

DIAMOND GRINDING HEADS Sized from 1/8" to 1".

GRINDING PLIERS Permits pieces of glass, even very small ones, to be moved onto the grinder.

BAND SAW This is used for difficult cutting.

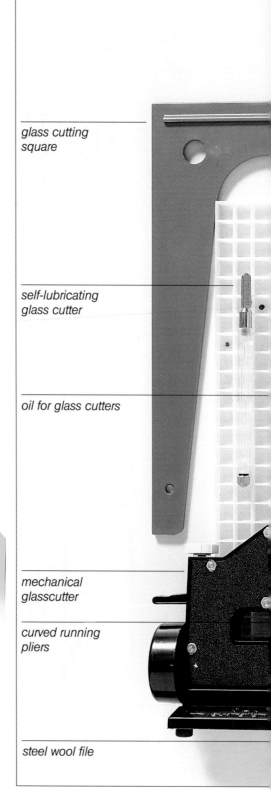

glass cutting square

self-lubricating glass cutter

oil for glass cutters

mechanical glasscutter

curved running pliers

steel wool file

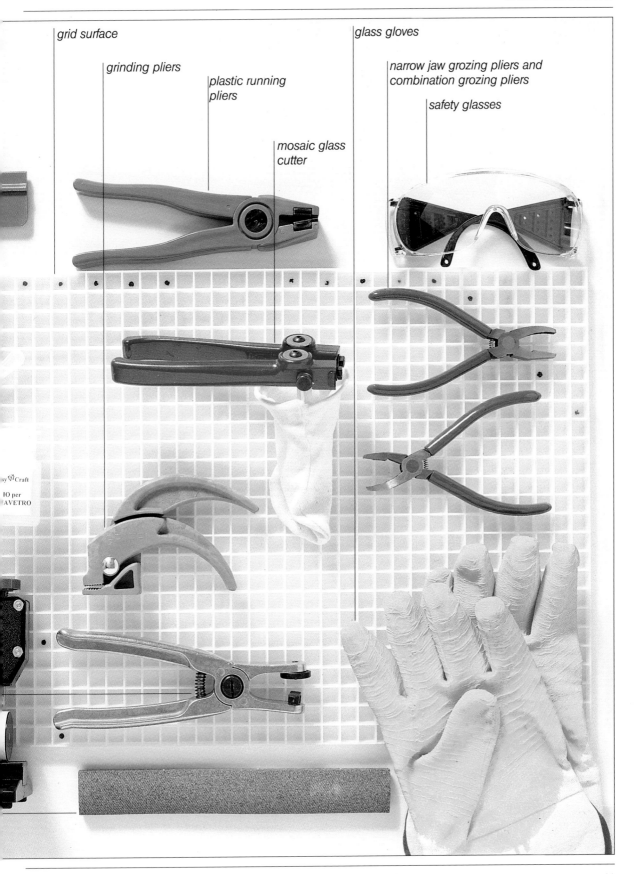

grid surface

grinding pliers

plastic running pliers

mosaic glass cutter

glass gloves

narrow jaw grozing pliers and combination grozing pliers

safety glasses

CUTTING, GROZING, AND GRINDING

Glass has always been viewed as a sharp and fragile material. It is natural that many beginners are inclined to handle it very warily for fear of hurting themselves. This chapter explains how to easily and safely use glass.

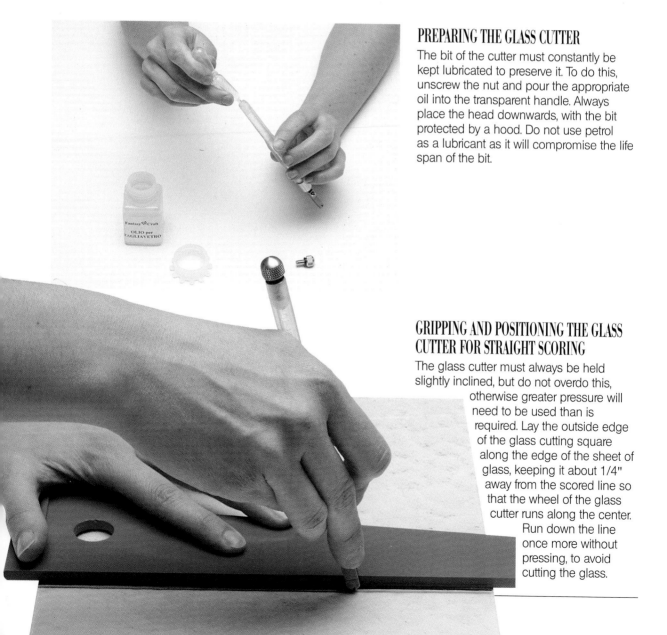

PREPARING THE GLASS CUTTER

The bit of the cutter must constantly be kept lubricated to preserve it. To do this, unscrew the nut and pour the appropriate oil into the transparent handle. Always place the head downwards, with the bit protected by a hood. Do not use petrol as a lubricant as it will compromise the life span of the bit.

GRIPPING AND POSITIONING THE GLASS CUTTER FOR STRAIGHT SCORING

The glass cutter must always be held slightly inclined, but do not overdo this, otherwise greater pressure will need to be used than is required. Lay the outside edge of the glass cutting square along the edge of the sheet of glass, keeping it about 1/4" away from the scored line so that the wheel of the glass cutter runs along the center. Run down the line once more without pressing, to avoid cutting the glass.

SCORING GLASS

Position the bit paying attention to the inclination of the cutter. Press and run along the scored line slowly and with a flowing movement from top to bottom. Do not use the cutter like a pencil. Bending your wrist will change the pressure which must remain unaltered along the whole run. Do not go over the scoring twice, as the cut will not improve and the cutter will be damaged.

USE OF BREAKER PLIERS TO BREAK STRAIGHT SCORES

The raised center on the jaws is placed under the sheet corresponding to the back of the scoring, while the jaw with the two raised parts on the side, is kept on top. Slip the pliers along the score as far as possible, matching the raised center with the scoring line. Without any movement of the pliers, press sharply on the handles to fracture the glass.

SCORING A GEOMETRICAL SHAPE

Lay the craft paper on the glass, then trace its perimeter with a marker. Score along the inside of the traced lines to get a glass piece the same size as the template. Regardless of the type of scoring, it must begin and end on the edges of the glass sheet. Simplify things by drawing the score line on the glass.

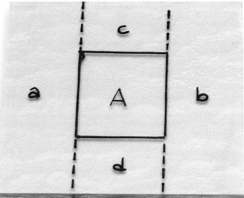

CUTTING THE GLASS PIECES

Remember to cut inside the marked lines of the glass pieces. First cut segment A, then B, and lastly C. With the breaker pliers subdivide the different sections.

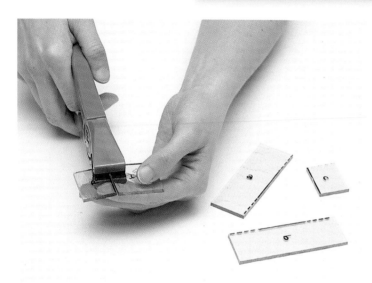

MATCHING THE GLASS PIECE AND THE TEMPLATE

Attach the template to the glass piece making sure they match perfectly. If the glass turns out to be bigger than the template, it will have to be ground until the two shapes are identical. If the glass is smaller, it will have to be reworked.

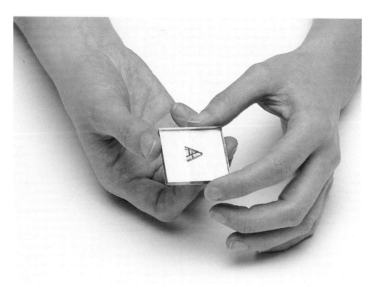

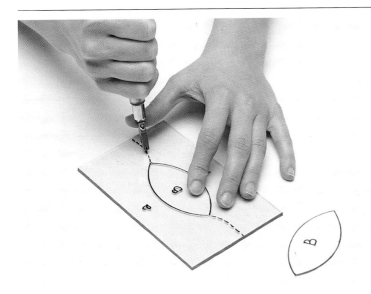

POSITIONING AND GRIPPING THE CUTTER FOR CURVED CUTTING

Trace the border of the paper template on the glass. Always keep the score line clearly visible. Cut from bottom to top. Grip the cutter almost vertically, with the thumb of the left hand placed behind the bit. With the wheel in the center of the mark, work slowly keeping the pressure even. First cut segment A, then B.

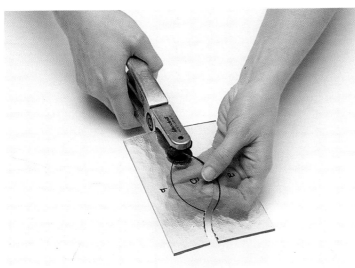

USING THE CURVED RUNNING PLIERS FOR CURVED CUTTING - 1

The jaw with the moving plastic segment must be placed towards the top and inclined perpendicularly to the score. The jaw with the protruding tip must be placed corresponding to the score. A sharp pressure on the handles will be enough to detach the glass along the scored line.

USING THE CURVED RUNNING PLIERS FOR CURVED CUTTING - 2

After having detached the first section of the glass, place the pliers on the B section line, remembering to keep the black segment perpendicular to the scoring line. Break the glass off and repeat with the other segments. To make breaking the glass easier, lightly tap on the back of the score with the nut of the cutter.

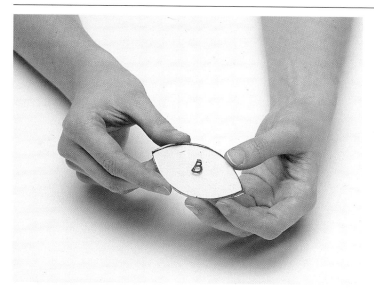

MATCHING THE GLASS PIECE AND THE TEMPLATE

Match the glass piece and the template making sure they correspond exactly.
If the glass is irregular or bigger than the template, grind it until the two shapes are identical.

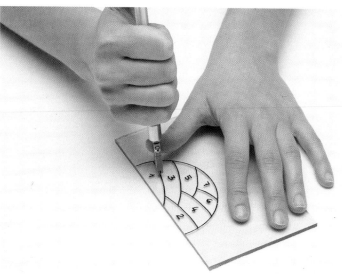

SCORING CONCAVE CURVES

If the scored curve is concave, the glass may break awkwardly. To avoid this, first score the curved line with a flowing run then make various scores in the concave part. Avoid carrying the score crossways on the external curved line.

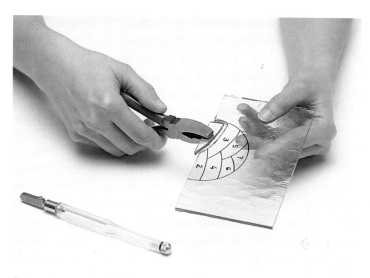

BREAKING OFF CONCAVE CURVES

To help break off the glass, lightly tap with the bolt of the cutter on the back of all the scored lines. Using wide jawed breaking pliers, grip the glass portions and snap off the piece. Begin from the outside section and repeat this procedure to the one furthest in. This is a very difficult cut to do. Therefore it is better to avoid curvatures that are too concave. Modify the design by lessening the depth or using other types of scoring.

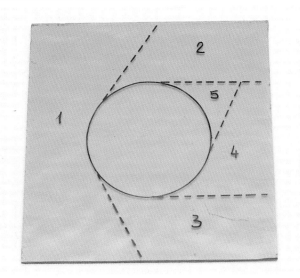

SCORING CONVEX CURVES

For convex curves, first score the whole curved line in one continuous flow, then make a number of scores at a tangent to the curvature. They must end at the edge of the sheet. Finish off the piece with the pliers or the grinder.

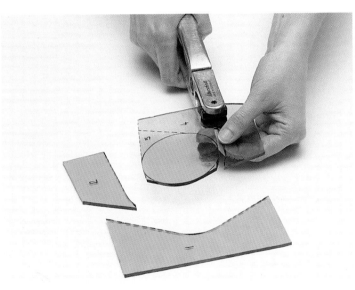

BREAKING OFF CONVEX CURVES

With the curved running pliers, grip the parts of glass outside the convex outline and with a sharp movement detach one piece at a time. Begin from the section marked with scores running from one part of the sheet to the other and then proceed with the remaining.

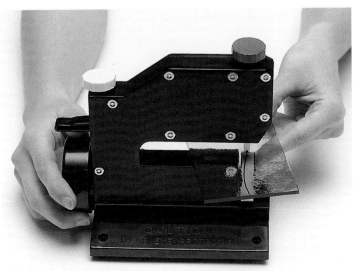

CUTTING WITH A MECHANICAL CUTTER

This is a very handy tool as it allows you to cut glass while seated. The pressure is kept constant by the cutter itself. First regulate the wheel for the thickness of the glass, and then the one which determines the pressure (use more pressure for harder pieces of glass). Lift the black lever and insert the glass under the cutter wheel. Block the glass by lowering the lever again. Turn the knob, letting the glass slide under the wheel. To break off the glass use the breaking pliers for straight or curved lines, according to the type of score made.

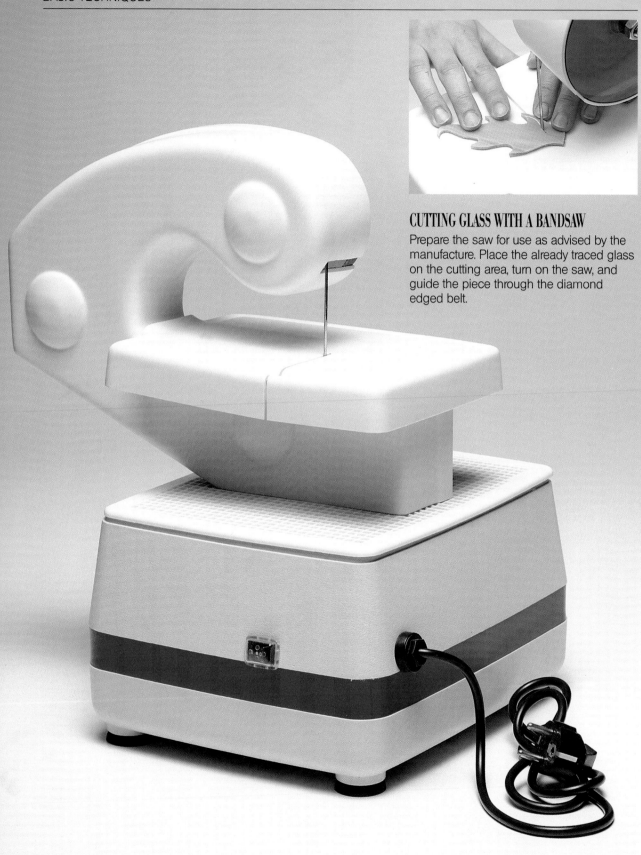

CUTTING GLASS WITH A BANDSAW

Prepare the saw for use as advised by the manufacture. Place the already traced glass on the cutting area, turn on the saw, and guide the piece through the diamond edged belt.

REMOVING UNEVEN PIECES WITH GROZING PLIERS

When the glass pieces are uneven, grozing pliers will eliminate unwanted fragments. Firmly grip the grozing pliers (combination or narrow jawed, according to the size of the fragments), hold the glass where it needs to be evened, and break the fragments off cleanly from top to bottom.

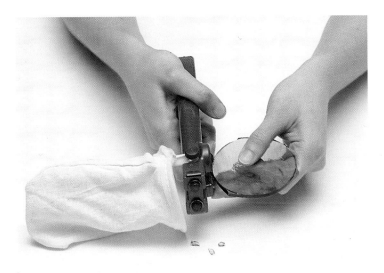

REMOVING UNEVEN PIECES USING A MOSSAIC GLASS CUTTER

Firmly grip the cutter and place the two wheels vertically to the uneven bits to be cut and press the handles. It is better to break off small sections of glass at a time so as not to cause irregular fractures.

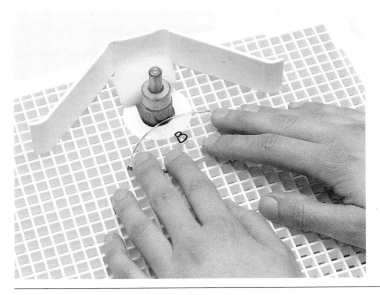

THE GRINDER - FINISHING

The grinder makes finishing cut glass pieces easier and more accurate. Turn the grinder on following the manufacture's instructions. Wear safety glasses to protect against splinters. Place the glass to be finished on the grid with the uneven parts pressed against the rotating diamond bit. Clean the glass and place it against the matching paper template to make sure it is identical.

PROJECTS

TIFFANY

This chapter will describe how to make a panel using the Tiffany technique, except for the steps relating to cutting glass. For this operation we advise those not yet sure of their skill to consult the chapter on cutting, grozing, and grinding glass. This panel, Asian in style and made up of a complex mixture of stylized vegetation, is entirely composed of cathedral glass. The green, yellow, and blue were industrially produced, while the red was made from craftsmen. Only transparent glass was chosen so as not to overburden the design, it being already quite complex. Soldering has been left natural and copper foil was used. The three most common widths are: 3/16" for the small pieces of glass, 7/32" for the medium sized, and 1/4" for the big ones. Zinc was used only for the yellow colored glass, which is mostly transparent. To satisfy composition needs, some parts of the panel were decorated with grisaille and baked in the furnace before being assembled. Given the complexity of the cutting and the high number of pieces involved (119), the Tiffany technique is the most suitable for this type of composition.

SOME TECHNICAL TIPS

— Only use suitable material, never leftovers. This is more practical, quicker, and safer.

— The secret of good cutting lies in correctly gripping the cutter and applying even pressure.

— Scrupulously trace the reference numbers and codes on every piece of glass.

— Do not underestimate any work phase. The slightest mistake at the beginning multiplies during each successive operation, which usually creates negative results in the end.

— From the moment of applying the foil and onwards, do not let too much time pass between each working phase. Oxidization of the metals could compromise the outcome of your work.

MORE EQUIPMENT

BURNISHING ROLLER
With its rotating roller in stiff rubber, this is used to burnish the copper foil to the cut glass pieces. It is particularly useful for medium and large sized pieces.

NYLON BURNISHER
This serves to make the copper foil adhere to the glass border. It is particularly useful for small sized templates.

HAND FOILER
This is to position and secure copper foil to glass pieces. The copper foil must enter the rod through the slot and come out through the roller at the end of the handle. The exiting foil is separated from the protecting paper and automatically centered on the glass.

FOILING MACHINE
Attach the edging machine to a wooden board. With this tool it is possible to apply the three most common sizes of copper foil and to keep the foil over and under the glass. The machine comes with three double rollers corresponding to the foil measurements: 3/16", 7/32", and 1/4".

FOIL CONTAINER BOX
This is useful for putting away the different sizes of copper foil.

SOLDERING IRON
This tool was especially created for this technique. It keeps the temperature under constant control. Its long-life galvanized tip, at an angle of 45°, is the best for soldering.

SOLDERING IRON STAND
This stand is designed to avoid accidental burning.

PATTERN SHEARS
These shears slice away a thin strip of paper, which represents the copper foil that will eventually be added in a later step. Thanks to this procedure, the glass panel will have the same dimensions as the original pattern.

WHITE PERMANENT MARKER FOR GLASS
The clear, compact color of this marker makes it visible on all types of glass, including white. It is waterproof and also resists grinding.

SAFETY SOLDERING MASK
This mask is very useful for protecting the airways when using irritants.

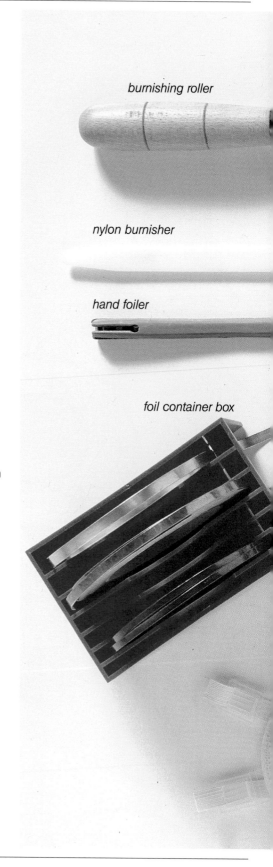

burnishing roller

nylon burnisher

hand foiler

foil container box

pattern shears

white permanent marker for glass

soldering iron stand

soldering iron

safety soldering mask

foiling machine

REQUIRED MATERIAL

COPPER FOIL
This comes in rolls with a thickness of .00125 mm and in various widths. It is strongly adhesive and resists high soldering temperatures. There are various types: copper backed (completely in copper), black backed copper (there is a black adhesive layer of zinc), and silver backed copper. The most common widths are: 3/16", 7/32", and 1/4".

COPPER RE-STRIP
This is a copper coil about 1/8" wide and 25 - 50 ft. long. It is inserted between the foiled pieces of glass and strengthens the panel structure.

SOLDER (63% TIN, 27% LEAD)
This is available in drawn rods. The solder must be of the best quality to avoid impurities that surface later and oxidize the seam surfaces.

FLUX BRUSH
This is used to brush on flux and the patinas. It does not corrode.

FLUX
This liquid, applied with a flux or small brush on the surface of the copper foil, eliminates oxidation and permits the melted solder to adhere perfectly.

SAL AMMONIAC
This cleans the tip of the soldering iron.

BLACK PATINA AND COPPER PATINA
Copper foil becomes a silver color when soldered. Patina modifies the silver coloring and creates, according to the type used, a thin black or copper, colored film on the solder.

PATINA REMOVER
This product is used to remove the thin black or copper colored film formed by the patinas. By rubbing the surface, the patina disappears and the tinplating returns to its original silver color.

FINISHING / CLEANING COMPOUND
When rubbed on natural soldering or seams with patina, this liquid makes them shine and protects them from oxidation and dampness.

WAX FOR GLASS
Wax makes the glass surface and soldering shine and protects them from dampness and dust.

copper foil

copper re-strip

solder

flux

Fantasy Craft
ACQUA SALDA

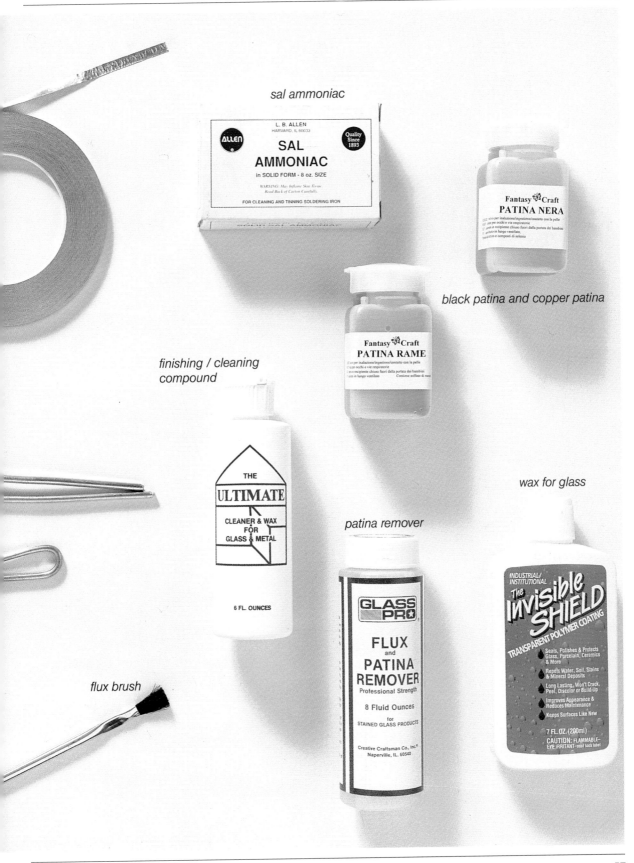

sal ammoniac

black patina and copper patina

finishing / cleaning
compound

wax for glass

patina remover

flux brush

MAKING A STAINED GLASS PANEL

REPRODUCING A SKETCH IN SCALE

Use a photocopier to reproduce the pattern on this page. Depending on the size you wish for your project, you can reproduce the pattern in the dimensions in which it is given, or enlarge it to the scale you desire. On a sturdy work surface, lay down a piece of smooth, medium-thick craft paper. Over it, place a piece of carbon paper. On top of both, place the reproduced pattern. With a pencil, trace the black outlines of the pattern carefully and thoroughly. When you are done, remove the top pattern and the carbon paper. Throw the carbon paper away. You will now have two copies of the pattern, one on thinner paper and one on thicker craft paper. The thicker one you'll cut out so that you have templates of each of the individual pieces of glass that comprise the whole panel; the other will remain intact, and will serve as a pattern on which you arrange the cut pieces of glass.

DETERMINING THE COLORS OF THE GLASS AND THE DIRECTION OF THE GLASS STRUCTURE

Following the different color tones, number every section with a letter of the alphabet corresponding to a certain color (A for red, B for green and so on). Remember to write down the color code. If you are using opalescent glass, mark some arrows on the pattern to show the direction of the glass. This will give the composition a better sense of plasticity and reality.

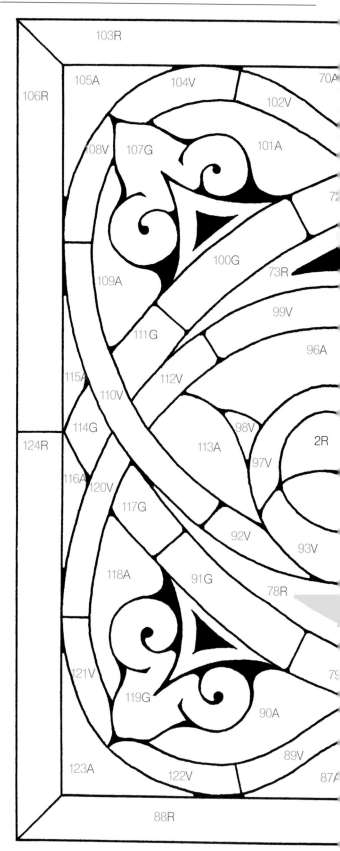

Glass color code: A = cathedral blue; G = cathedral yellow; R = cathedral red; V = cathedral green.

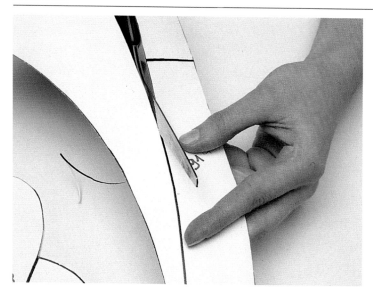

CUTTING THE PAPER TEMPLATES

Cut the border of the pattern outside the black line. Use ordinary scissors. Use the pattern shears to cut the numbered templates. Properly grip the shears, positioning the single blade upwards. Cut, following the pattern line, along the middle. Cut slowly and with small snips, first dividing the craft paper in large sections, then in smaller ones until you reach the individual templates.

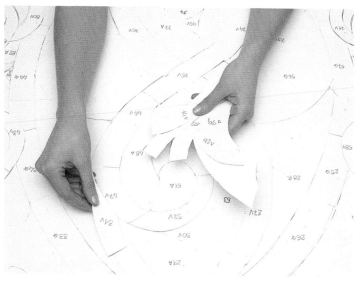

RECOMPOSING THE PAPER PUZZLE

After having cut all the templates, they will have to be reassembled following the soldering seam, as per the numbers given. What turns out at the end is a craft paper puzzle. During the successive working phases we shall substitute each paper template with its corresponding piece of cut colored glass.

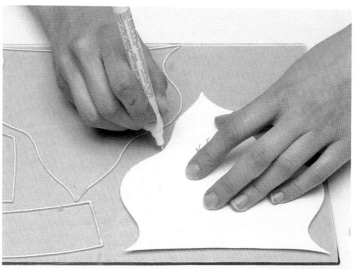

DESIGNING THE PATTERN ON GLASS

Subdivide the templates according to the color of the glass. Place the templates on the relative glass then reproduce their outline and number with a fine-tipped white glass marker. Begin cutting, grozing, and grinding all the glass, as indicated on pages 42-49.

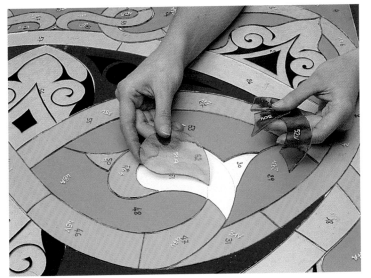

RECOMPOSING AND CHECKING THE GLASS PIECES

As the pieces of glass are cut out one after another, lay them on the soldering seam with the help of the numbers you have given them. Check that the cut glass piece and the space it should occupy are the same. Should there be any imprecision, re-grind or re-cut the piece. Also grind any glass that is too sharp, which might cause wounds while putting on the copper foil. Make sure that no piece of glass jams another and that sufficient space has been left for the copper foil and for soldering.

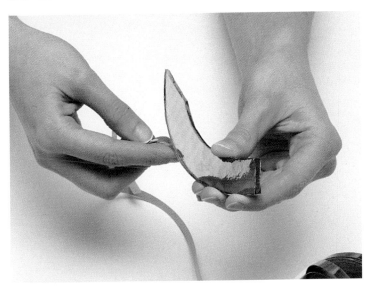

EDGING WITH COPPER FOIL

Apply the copper foil to the glass edge little by little. Superimpose about 1/8" of foil at the starting point and then cut with scissors. Bend in and flatten the coil all along the edges.

BURNISHING THE COPPER FOIL

To make the copper foil adhere to the glass, press it with the roller or the nylon burnisher along both sides of the traced line. Instead of applying the copper foil manually, the foiling machine may be used to save time.

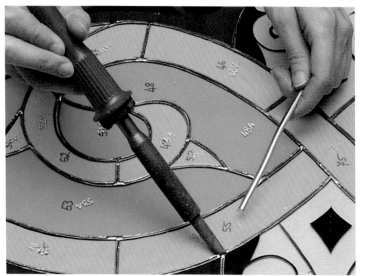

SOLDERING ON THE FRONT PANEL

The pattern of the panel is now completed. Soldering must de done within one or two days because the copper foil could oxidize and damage the work. Before the actual soldering is carried out, join the glass pieces with little dabs of soldering to prevent them from moving by mistake. Brush on the flux where the various pieces of glass touch each other. With the hot soldering iron, pick up and then deposit a small quantity of solder.

FULL SOLDERING ON THE FRONT PANEL

When the glass pieces have been blocked in position, soldering must then fill in the spaces. Brush flux over short lengths of the soldering. Gradually melt the solder and deposit it, little by little, in the grooves until they are filled.

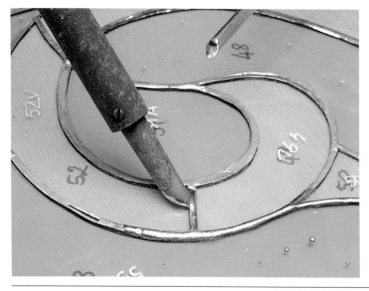

BEADED SOLDERING ON THE FRONT PANEL

Brush flux once more over the soldered seams and then evenly deposit more solder until it is rounded in shape. The tip of the soldering iron must be fully pressed as it solders. Besides being attractive, beaded soldering also helps to strengthen the panel structure.

FLAT SOLDERING ON THE REAR PANEL

Deposit a small amount of solder along the whole soldering line keeping it stretched out flat, not rounded. The solder must be maintained as liquid so that it can flow easily. Only in this way will the soldering be smooth and without peaks. Should some solder drip on the back of the panel, wait for the soldering to cool and then clean it.

SOLDERING THE BORDER

This operation is carried out on small sized panels not intended to be in a structure and on those that the border will remain visible. Raise the panel and make sure the side is held perfectly horizontal. Working from left to right, deposit small quantities of solder.

CLEANING THE PANEL

Clean the work with a cloth dipped in a finishing compound, and then dry carefully. Pour a few drops of polishing cream on a clean cotton cloth and rub over the soldering. Leave to dry and then, with another clean cloth, rub again until the soldering and the glass shine. If you would like to give the soldering a patina, do not let more then an hour or two pass. Clean with a cloth dipped in a solution of water and 20% ammonia or a finishing compound. Dry and rub over the soldering with a cloth dipped in a patina.

TRADITIONAL

This technique is very easy and produces very elegant work. This particular work is attached to a leaded glass background of simple and linear structure, and is an elaborate central panel decorated with grisaille (details of this technique are on page 114). Cathedral glass in light tones of yellow and green are used in this panel to highlight the central composition. Furthermore, the Victorian style leading of the structure has been purposely simplified to avoid taking the attention away from the main subject. The central part, in cathedral glass, was first carefully shaped and tried within the framework of the composition, then decorated with grisaille. At this point it was leaded with the other glass pieces. Beginners to this technique are advised to grade the difficulty of the work as they proceed. To work safely, it is essential to allot a corner of one's home to this activity and to have a working table where tools and materials can be left during breaks from work.

SOME TECHNICAL TIPS

— Choose relatively easy patterns. Leaded glass pieces must be somewhat large.
— Beginners should use patterns created for this particular technique.
— Do not use too much solder and only solder at the intersecting points.
— Use tools and materials specifically made for this activity. If the soldering iron is not of good quality, it will melt not only the solder but also the lead.
— Do not let too much time pass between soldering and applying a patina.
— Wash your hands carefully after using lead.

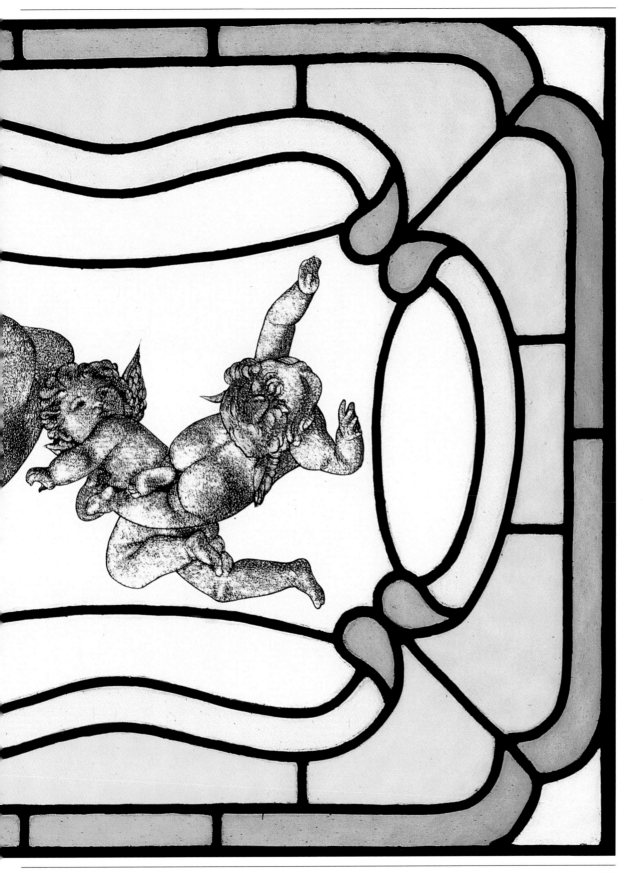

MORE EQUIPMENT

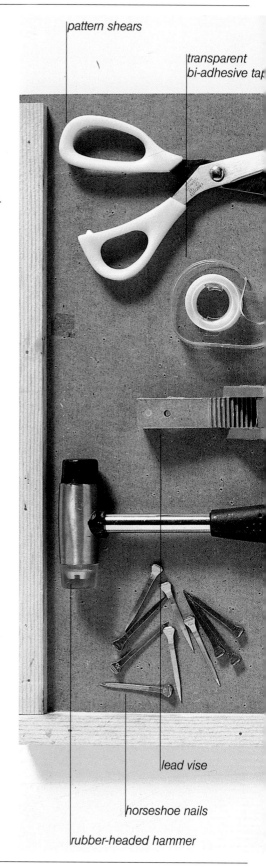

PATTERN SHEARS
These shears, used for cutting the paper templates, slice away a thin strip of about 1/16" and thus reduce the size of the template. The increased space is then filled with lead came.

TRANSPARENT BI-ADHESIVE TAPE
This is used to secure the soldering trace to the worktable.

LEAD VISE
This serves to straighten the lead came, which is extremely delicate.

HORSESHOE NAILS
These nails damage lead less than other types and can easily be taken out.

RUBBER-HEADED HAMMER
A light, handy hammer is needed to hammer in the horseshoe nails and straighten the came.

LATHEKIN
This is made from strong nylon and is used to straighten and open up the lead came so that the glass may be inserted easily.

LEAD CAME KNIFE
The lead came can be easily cut with this.

COPPER RE-STRIP
This is a copper coil 1/8" wide and 25-50 ft. long. It is inserted between the foiled pieces of glass and strengthens the panel structure.

SOLDERING IRON
This is regulated to control the solder temperature accurately and continuously.

SOLDERING IRON STAND
This helps to avoid accidental burns.

GLOVES
These are used when puttying or cementing.

STEEL SPATULA
This is used to place the cement into the lead came.

CEMENT / SCRUB BRUSH
This is used to clean the panel.

WORK TABLE WITH HOLDING LATHS
The worktable should be made of multi-layered wood so that it can easily take nails and so that it will not become distorted with dampness.

pattern shears

transparent bi-adhesive tape

lead vise

horseshoe nails

rubber-headed hammer

lathekin

lead came
knife

copper re-strip

cement /
scrub brush

worktable with
holding laths

soldering iron stand

steel spatula

gloves

soldering iron

REQUIRED MATERIAL

"U" AND "H" SHAPED LEAD CAME
To join the glass pieces together, they must be inserted into and then secured in lead channels called lead came. This usually comes in rods of 2 to 3 yards in various widths. There are two types of lead came, "U" shaped, which is used around the border of the panel, and "H" shaped, which is used internally to assemble the different pieces of glass.

PUTTY
This patented product is ready for use and does not need other elements added. As it hardens it seals the came perfectly, yet remains elastic enough to give flexibility to the panel. Drying time depends on room temperature. It is better to clean the putty immediately after it has been applied.

SOLDER (63% TIN, 27% LEAD)
This is available in drawn rods. The solder must be of the best quality to avoid impurities that may surface later and oxidize the soldering. Avoid solder used for electrical joining, or worse, for plumbing. Even though they are cheaper, they are difficult to work with.

FLUX
This liquid is a de-oxidizer which, when brushed on the lead came surface, eliminates oxidation and allows the melted solder to adhere perfectly.

FLUX BRUSH
This is used to brush on flux and patinas.

SAWDUST
Fine-grained sawdust absorbs any oily flux excess and cleans the glass, leaving it shiny.

BLACK PATINA
Black patina is used to modify the silver color of the solder, making it the same color as the came. The came would otherwise oxidize and become darker and more opaque than the solder. The liquid patina sets off a chemical reaction on the soldered surface and creates a thin black film. Do not use copper patina because it reacts only to solder and not to lead.

FINISHING COMPOUND
This finishing cleaner, for soldering and patinas, leaves the lead came and soldering shining and also protects them from oxidation and dampness.

WAX FOR GLASS
Wax makes the surface of glass and soldering shine, and preserves them from dampness and dust.

"U" and "H" shaped lead came

putty

flux brush

flux

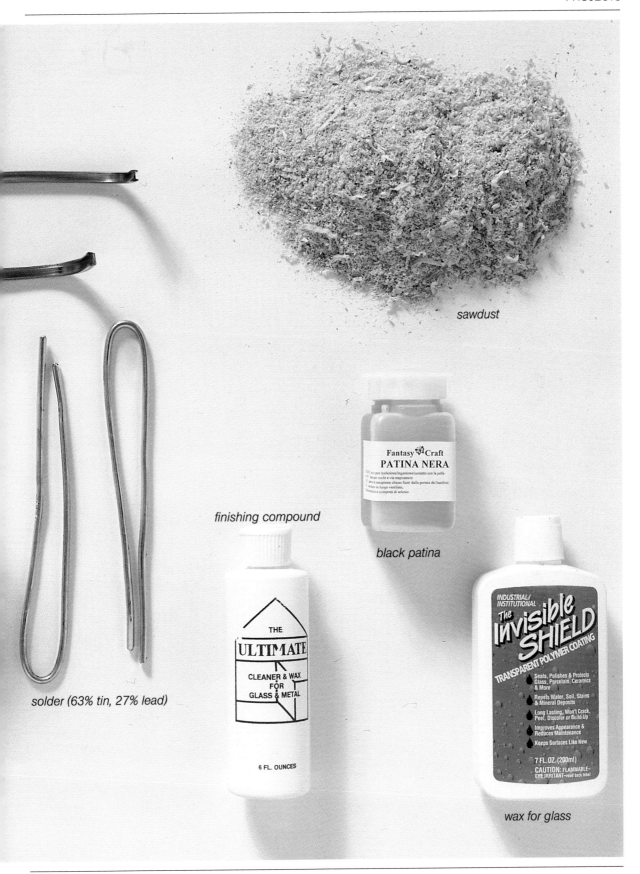

sawdust

finishing compound

black patina

solder (63% tin, 27% lead)

wax for glass

MAKING A STAINED GLASS PANEL

REPRODUCING A SKETCH IN SCALE

Use a photocopier to reproduce the pattern on this page. Depending on the size you wish for your project, you can reproduce the pattern in the dimensions in which it is given, or enlarge it to the scale you desire. On a sturdy work surface, lay down a piece of smooth, medium-thick craft paper. Over it, place a piece of carbon paper. On top of both, place the reproduced pattern. With a pencil, trace the black outlines of the pattern carefully and thoroughly. When you are done, remove the top pattern and the carbon paper. Throw the carbon paper away. You will now have two copies of the pattern, one on thinner paper and one on thicker craft paper. The thicker one you'll cut out so that you have templates of each of the individual pieces of glass that comprise the whole panel; the other will remain intact, and will serve as a pattern on which you arrange the cut pieces of glass.

DETERMINING THE COLOR AND DIRECTION OF THE GLASS STRUCTURE

Reproduce the prepared pattern on smooth craft paper. Use a medium sized black felt pen and try to be as accurate as possible. Also reproduce on the craft paper the same numbers as indicated on the soldering lines. Mark each section with a letter of the alphabet. Each mark must correspond to a given color (T for transparent, V for Green, etc.). Remember to write down the color code on a sheet of paper. If you are using opalescent glass, mark each piece of glass with an arrow to indicate the direction of the glass. (See Collage Glass, step 2) This operation is not necessary when transparent glass such as cathedral glass is used, as this does not have streaks.

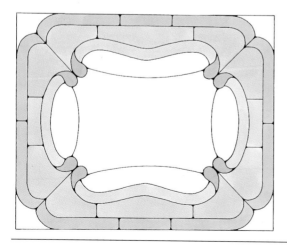

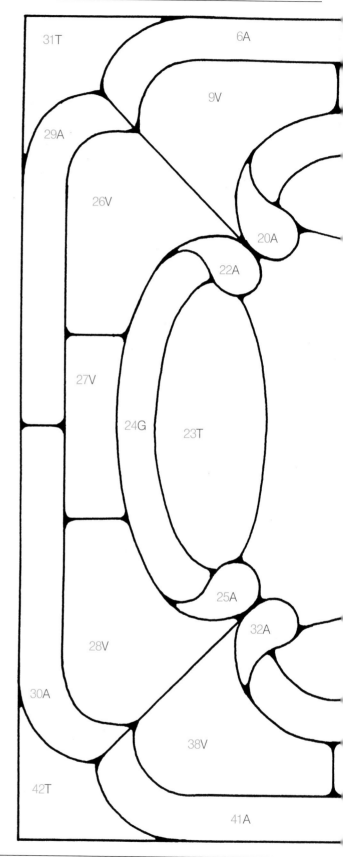

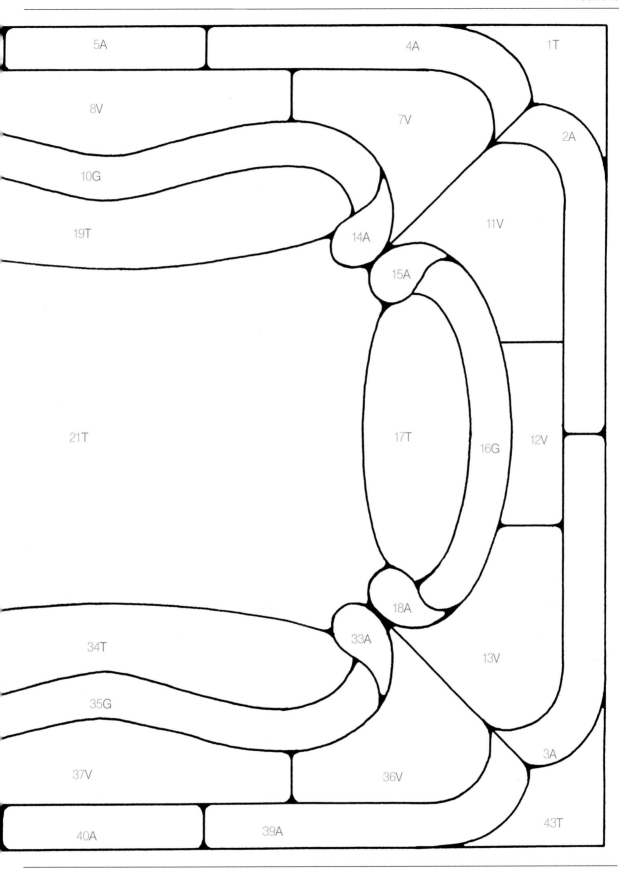

Color code: A = dark yellow; G = Yellow; T = transparent; V = green.

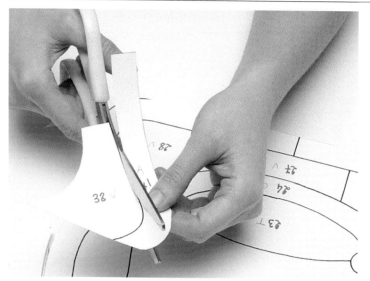

CUTTING THE TEMPLATES

Cut the border out of the craft paper using ordinary scissors. To cut the numbered inside templates, use the pattern shears (these are not the same as those used for the Tiffany technique). These scissors slice away a thin strip of paper of about 1/16", thus reducing the size of the paper template, and also of the glass one. Gripping the scissors with the single blade facing upwards, cut slowly in short lengths following the middle part of the pattern line. This operation is necessary because by adding the thickness of the lead came, the panel will be bigger than the original pattern.

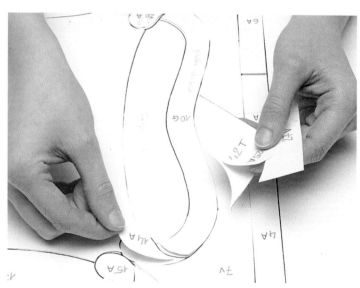

REASSEMBLING THE PAPER PUZZLE

Follow the numbered coding and reassemble the cut out templates on the soldering line. The result is a paper puzzle.

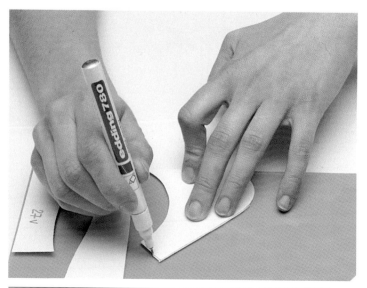

DESIGNING THE PATTERN ON THE GLASS

Divide the paper puzzle templates according to the numbered coding. Begin with one piece of glass and place it over the corresponding colored template (where the glass is opalescent be sure to place them with the arrow pointing in the direction of the glass). With a fine-pointed white glass marker, outline the paper pieces on the glass and reproduce the same numbers that are on the template. Cut all the various pieces of glass, as shown on pages 42-49.

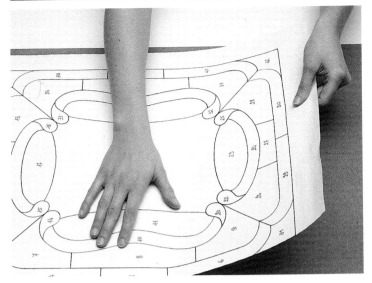

PLACING THE SOLDERING TRACE ON THE WORK TABLE

Obtain a multi-layered wooden board slightly bigger than the glass panel. Nail two wooden laths at right angles to each other on the board. They will hold the panel in alignment during assembly. With ordinary scissors, cut two sides of the soldering trace line. To prevent the pattern from slipping during work, stick bi-adhesive tape on the four corners on the back of the pattern. Secure the pattern to the board and match the two sides, without edges, to the alignment laths.

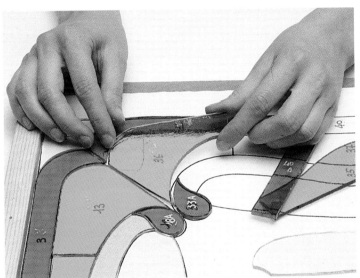

REASSEMBLING THE GLASS PUZZLE

As you cut the glass, place the pieces on the soldering line. Be sure that the pieces are identical to the spaces with the corresponding numbers. If there are any irregularities correct them with the grinder. If this is not possible then the pieces must be reworked. When the puzzle is finished, check that no piece of glass is in the way of another and that there is space for the came. Where necessary, make any other adjustments.

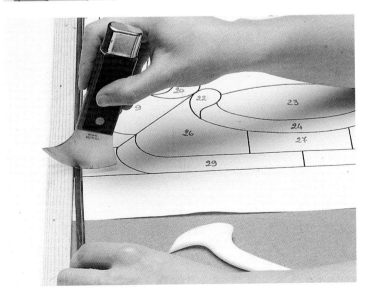

CUTTING THE LEAD CAME BORDER SEGMENTS

Now we will proceed to leading the panel. Take a segment of the "U" shaped came the same length as the long side of the panel and, trying not to twist it, lay it on the wooden board along the lath. To mark the size, make a notch with the lead came knife. Place the lead came with one of the two segments of the "U" on the table, keeping it firm. Press lightly but firmly until the lead is cut. Try not to damage the lead or bend the flanges.

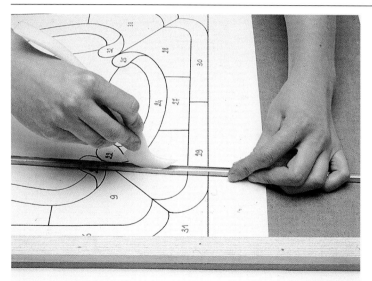

OPENING AND STRAIGHTENING THE LEAD CAME

If the lead came has been bent, proceed as follows: lay the rod on the table with its flanges upwards, insert the lathekin, and lightly run it along the channel opening up the furrow. Check that the came rod is straight and not twisted anywhere.

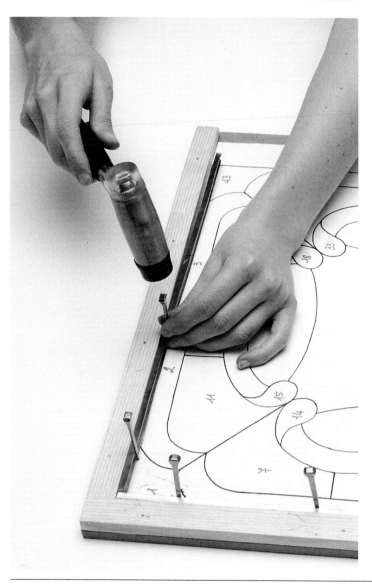

SECURING SEGMENTS ONE AND TWO OF "U" CAME WITH HORSESHOE NAILS

Place the lead came along the lath and with the lathekin run along the channel, pressing firmly and making sure that it adheres perfectly. In order to keep the came in position, begin from the top and secure it with some nails being careful not to stick them in the lead. Cut the segment of lead came that will secure the adjoining side. Measure from the border of the already secured lead came to the border of the design. The two pieces of lead came in the corner are not to be overlapped, but merely joined. Secure this segment with some horseshoe nails.

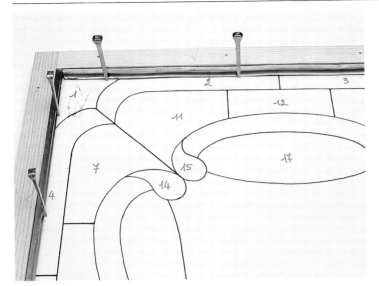

ORDER OF INSERTING THE GLASS PIECES

It is now time to secure the glass pieces of the panel and to decide on the order to follow. It is important to always leave the way out clear. There is obviously no standard order, but it varies according to the pattern. In our case this is the order to follow: first insert glass 1, then 2, 3, 4, 5, 6. Always mark the order of the numbers directly on the soldering line.

INSERTING THE FIRST PIECE OF GLASS

Now take the various, previously cut glass pieces and choose the numbers to fit in first. Take out the horseshoe nails near where you will be working and then pass the lathekin along the lead came. Fit the number "1" piece of glass delicately in the corner. Secure the glass with some nails. It is very important to use horseshoe nails, as other pieces can be assembled only if the preceding ones are firmly in place and do not move.

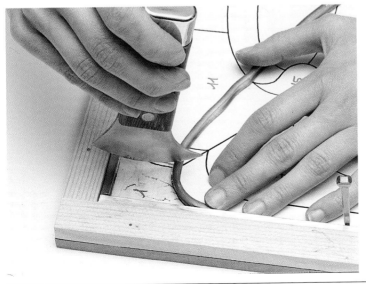

USE OF "H" LEAD CAME AND SECURING WITH NAILS

Cut a segment of lead came about 20" from the main rod. Place one end on the lath, making a notch with the knife to indicate where the came is to be cut. To cut the H-shaped came, place the knife on the mark and press firmly. If the flanges are a little bent, open them with the lathekin. Let the lead came slide delicately under the glass. When it is positioned, make a notch with the knife to mark the point where the lead came is to be cut. Make the cut about 1/8" before the end of the glass to allow the other lead came to be inserted.

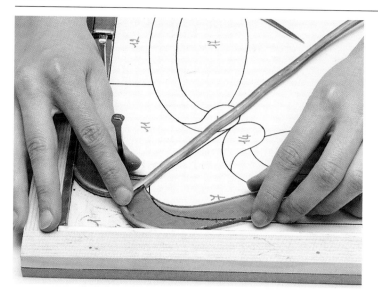

INSERTING THE OTHER GLASS PIECES

Now proceed with glass piece number "2" and so on until the whole panel has been completed.

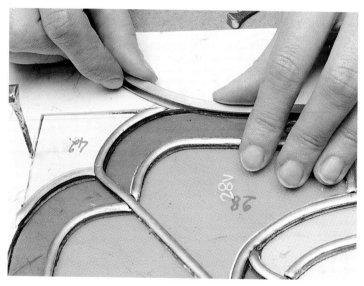

FINISHING THE PANEL WITH TWO OUTER BORDERS

When all the glass pieces have been inserted according to the code, the panel must be finished off with two outer borders. Cut a segment of the "U" lead came equal to the long side of the panel. Open the channel and straighten out any twists. Extract the first horseshoe nails and insert the lead came under the glass. Secure the first part with some horseshoe nails, take out the remaining nails, and insert the rest of the lead came. Again, hold in position with some nails. Proceed in the same way for the other border.

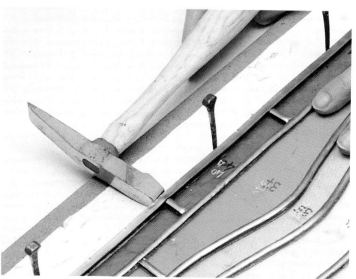

COMPACTING THE PANEL

As can be seen on the border, the nails have not been placed corresponding to the intersecting pieces of lead came. This is to allow for the compacting of the panel and subsequent soldering. Lightly tap the lead came with the hammer, particularly on the protruding parts until the border of the panel is perfectly aligned. Do not press the lead on the glass or otherwise the putty will have difficulty entering.

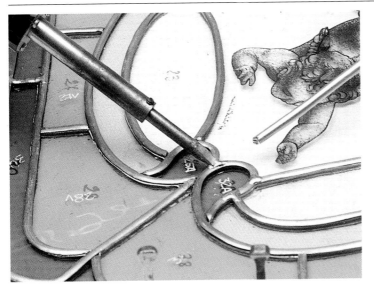

SOLDERING THE BORDER AND INTERNAL POINTS

Brush the various intersecting points between the lead came with flux, only working in small areas so as to solder quickly. Using the hot soldering iron, pick up a small dab of solder and deposit it on the contact points of the lead. Lay the tip of the soldering iron flat and make a slight circular movement to widen the soldering. The solder rod should not be more than 1/8" from the tip of the iron to avoid drops from falling on the glass. Follow the same procedure for soldering the border.

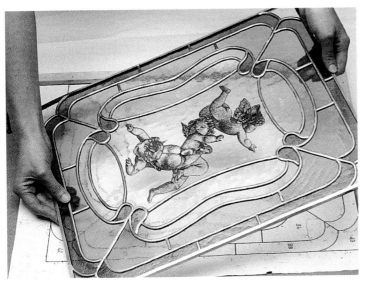

REMOVING HORSESHOE NAILS AND SOLDERING THE REAR PART

Once the front soldering has been completed remove all the horseshoe nails and begin the rear soldering. Pass the iron and a little solder on all the various intersecting points between the lead came. Proceed to the front part of the panel. During this step, try to avoid drips on the back of the panel by lingering too long on one spot with the iron.

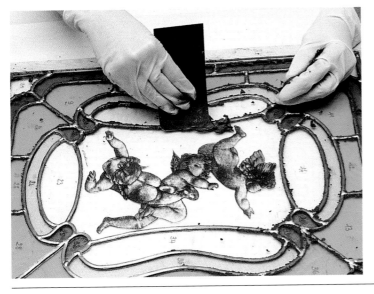

PUTTYING THE STAINED GLASS

Clear the worktable of the soldering gear to prepare for the next step, puttying the panel. With gloves on, open the tin of putty and extract a little with the spatula. Slide the putty under the lead came, delicately and without disturbing the lead, with the spatula. First pass from one part of the lead came and then to the other. Continue in this way for the entire project, including the border. Turn the panel over and repeat this step on the rear part as well.

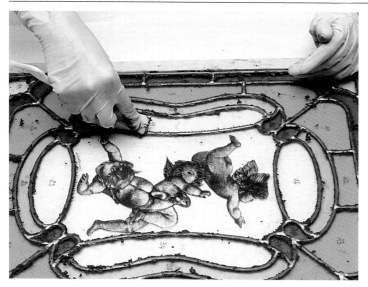

CLOSING THE LEAD CAME AND CLEANING THE PUTTY

When the puttying is finished, pass the lathekin over the whole traced line of lead closing the flanges on the glass, including the putty inside. Clean off the putty with the lathekin and get rid of the excess material. Careful cleaning is not necessary since it will later be done with sawdust. Turn the panel over and repeat on the rear part as well.

CLEANING WITH SAWDUST

Get some ordinary sawdust and throw it all over the panel. Rub it over the glass and the lead came with your hands. The sawdust will get rid of all traces of putty and its oils, and will leave the glass sparkling clean.

USING THE SCRUB / CEMENT BRUSH

When cleaning with sawdust it is a good idea to use a scrub or cement brush. Pass it over the whole panel in a circular movement without pressing too hard so as not to scrape the lead, which is a very soft metal. When this is done use a cotton cloth to eliminate the dust. Turn the panel over and repeat on the rear part as well. Check the panel against the light to see if any traces of putty remain, and if they do take them off with a wooden stick.

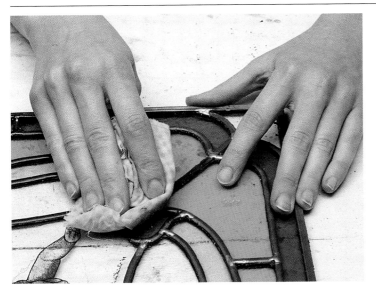

APPLYING A PATINA

To eliminate traces of sawdust use a cloth dipped in a solution of 20% ammonia and water or a finishing compound. If you would like to match the silver color of the soldering to the color of the came, rub on the black patina. Using a small cloth dipped in black patina rub the liquid onto the lead and soldering until they become a dark shade.

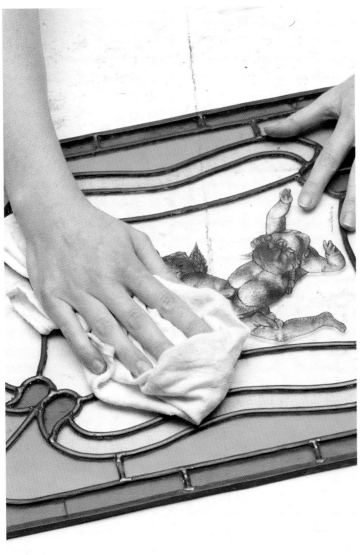

POLISHING AND WAXING

To make the soldering and lead shine, pour a few drops of polishing cream on a clean cotton cloth and rub it lightly over the work. Let it to dry a minute and then rub it with another clean cloth. To wax the panel, pour a few drops of wax on the glass including the solder. The panel must be left to completely dry for at least an hour. Finish with a good rub using a clean cloth. The panel will be covered with a thin film, which will protect it from dust and dampness.

COLLAGE

This chapter will explain how to make a panel to insert into a table. A panel made with this technique is very robust and the surface turns out perfectly smooth and free from traces of soldering, as well as being completely waterproof. A pattern of tropical flowers and toucans, covering the whole panel, was decided on. The glass is exclusively opalescent to prevent seeing under the table. The background, almost completely covered by the subject, is of petrol blue opalescent glass. To differentiate between the species, greens of various types and shades were used. For the flowers and toucans we opted for a real explosion of bright, lively colors. The transparent supporting glass is 1/8" thick and withstands weight. The pattern shown could be enlarged if you would like to use it in a different context.

SOME TECHNICAL TIPS

— Before arranging the frame, check to make sure that the structure can hold it. If a door is in question, for example, make sure that; the laths are completely hidden by the door's frame, that there is space enough for the thickness of the glass, and that the frame itself can withstand the weight.

— For this technique the grinder must be used, particularly the fine-grained, diamond-coated bit of 3/4" for mirrors and chamfers, which provides the necessary angle for grinding.

— Resin-glass was made specifically for use with any sort of glass, but it is not advisable to use other, non-suitable products, as they lose with time the necessary characteristics of purity and transparency.

— Only prepare the required amount of Resin-glass, as once mixed it cannot be preserved.

MORE EQUIPMENT

(Besides the basic equipment for cutting and grinding glass)

PATTERN SHEARS
(TIFFANY TECHNIQUE)
These shears are used to cut craft paper patterns, as they
slice off a thin strip of paper.

3/4" FINE-GRAINED DIAMOND BIT FOR MIRRORS
This is useful for giving the proper angle to the edges of the glass.

PERMANENT MARKER FOR GLASS
Its clear, compact mark shows up on all types of glass including
white glass. It is waterproof and even resists grinding. Always
make sure to use it in a vertical position and never to press the tip.

SAFETY MASK FOR SOLDERING
This protects the airways when irritants are used.

SAFETY GLOVES
Use rubber gloves when mixing and working with Resin-glass.

DIGITAL SCALE
This is essential for accurately mixing the Resin-glass elements.

PLASTIC CONTAINER WITH WOODEN SPOON
This is for mixing the Resin-glass components.

STEEL SPATULA WITH WOODEN HANDLE
This cleans off the dried Resin-glass.

REQUIRED MATERIAL

RESIN-GLASS
This is a patented product created for use with all types of glass.
It is made of a transparent base and an activator, which hardens
the mixture. The two products are to be mixed in the proportions
of 100:45.

BI-ADHESIVE TRANSPARENT TAPE
This serves to secure the alignment laths to the glass base.

WIDE ADHESIVE TAPE
This isolates the glass base from the liquid discharge of the
Resin-glass.

WAX SHIELD
This isolates the upper part of the glass from the Resin-glass.

WAX FOR GLASS
Wax makes glass surfaces and soldering bright and shiny.

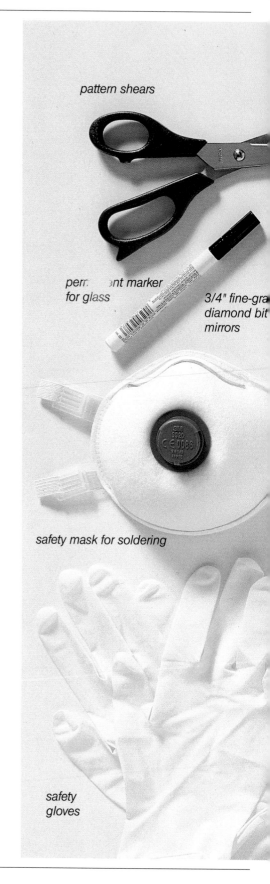

pattern shears

*permanent marker
for glass*

*3/4" fine-grained
diamond bit for
mirrors*

safety mask for soldering

*safety
gloves*

digital scale

bi-adhesive
transparent tape

Fantasy Craft
RESIN - GLASS 1

resin-glass

wax shield

MELTONIAN
Shoe Cream

Fantasy Craft
**RESIN - GLASS 2
(ATTIVATORE)
Corrosivo**

plastic container with
wooden spoon

wide adhesive tape

The
Invisible
SHIELD
TRANSPARENT POLYMER COATING

steel spatula with wooden
handle

wax for glass

MAKING THE PANEL

REPRODUCING THE PATTERN TO SCALE (DESIGNING - TRACING)

As with Tiffany and traditional stained glass, collage must also be sketched or reproduced to full size. Add about 1/16" to the outer rim of the four sides (mark the limit of the pattern with a red mark). This added dimension is needed for adding glass rods. The transparent frame formed by the rods, or laths, will be hidden by the structure holding the panel. Tracing this design will show the exact size where each glass piece must be during the assembly stage. Number every section from top to bottom outlined in the pattern.

TRANSFERRING THE PATTERN TO CRAFT PAPER, NUMBERING, AND DETERMINING THE COLORS AND DIRECTION OF THE GLASS STRUCTURE

Reproduce the pattern full size on smooth craft paper, tracing only the pattern inside the transparent frame (red mark). Transfer to the paper the same numbers as traced. For the color code, see the panel photo on page 81. Remember to write down the color code on a sheet of paper. Should the glass be opalescent and therefore streaked, mark arrows on the pattern to show the direction of the panel.

Opalescent glass code:
petrol blue (background)
medium green
moss green
pink
pale yellow
orange
red
light blue
brown
dark gray
black

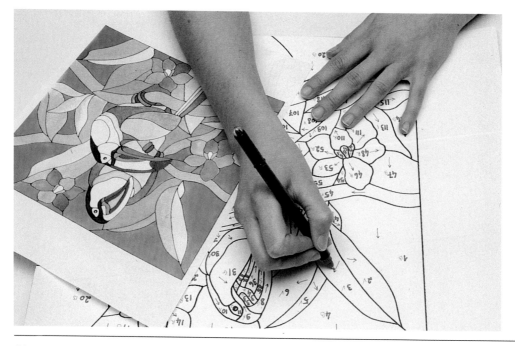

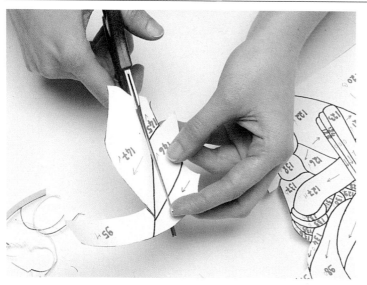

CUTTING THE TEMPLATES

Cut out the whole pattern using ordinary scissors. To cut out the numbered templates use the pattern shears. Direct the single blade upwards, and cut along the middle of the pattern line. These shears slice off a thin strip of paper. The size of the glass pieces must be reduced a little for them to be inserted into the frame.

RECOMPOSING THE TEMPLATE PUZZLE

Cut out all the paper templates and place them on the traced design according to the prearranged numbering. The result will be a paper puzzle.

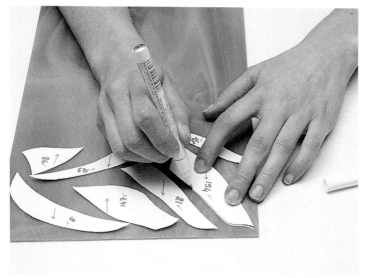

CUTTING THE GLASS

Subdivide the paper templates according to the color of the glass. Place the templates on the glass making sure that the arrow runs in the direction of the streaks in the glass. Reproduce the outlines and numbers with a white marker for glass. Now start cutting all the glass pieces. This requires a high grade of precision since the glass pieces remain fully visible. Because there is no border, the space between each piece of glass must be the same thickness as the whole panel. Grind all the glass pieces with a grinding bit for mirrors.

PREPARING THE SUPPORTING GLASS

Prepare a panel of transparent glass corresponding to the size of the traced pattern. The thickness of the glass must be in direct proportion to the size of the glass—the greater the size, the greater the thickness. You can start from a minimum of 1/16" for small panels, 1/8" for medium sized panels, and progressively increase. Wrap transparent bi-adhesive tape around the whole border of the base.

ATTACHING GLASS LATHS TO THE BORDER WITH BI-ADHESIVE TAPE

Prepare four glass laths 3/4" wide (one for each side of the base). Position the end part precisely 3/4" from the adjoining side and cut off the excess with the cutter. Repeat this procedure for the three other laths. Our panel pattern measures 12 1/2" x 12 1/2", the supporting panel measures 12 1/2" x 15 3/6", and the cut laths measure 3/4" x 12 9/16". The supporting glass is 1/8" thick.

REASSEMBLING THE GLASS PUZZLE

Put the tracing pattern under the supporting glass. The part with the pattern must correspond exactly with the space inside the glass laths. Place the cut and ground glass pieces inside the supporting glass. Check that the cut glass pieces match their spaces exactly and that the spaces between the glass pieces are uniform.

ISOLATING THE SUPPORTING GLASS WITH MASKING TAPE

Transfer the glass pieces beside your working space onto a copy of the pattern. Lay the traced pattern behind the supporting glass. Cover it completely with masking tape to protect it from the Resin-glass.

ISOLATING THE GLASS PIECES WITH WAX

Resin-glass in its liquid state is very adhesive and cannot be removed once it is stuck to glass. Therefore, the upper part of the glass pieces must be well isolated because during the work they are completely covered by the resin. Pick up some wax on your index finger and rub it over the outward facing surface of each glass. Reassemble the glass pieces on the traced pattern with the waxed part facing up. Also, isolate with wax the surface of the glass border laths secured to the supporting glass.

PREPARING THE RESIN-GLASS

You must pay close attention from this moment on since the next steps must be followed with the utmost precision and speed. The resins remain liquid for 15-20 minutes after which they become sticky and tend to solidify. Put the empty and perfectly clean container on the weighing scales, pour in the base of the Resin-glass up to the prearranged quantity, and add the correct dose of the activator.

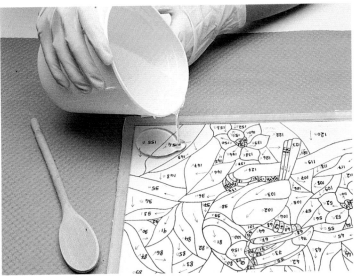

POURING THE RESIN-GLASS

Mix the two components without whipping so as not to create bubbles. Beginning from the top of the frame, pour a little of the product and move it around with your hand.

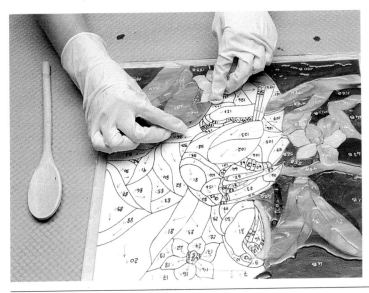

ARRANGING THE CUT GLASS PIECES

Arrange the glass pieces one at a time inside the frame, inserting them in the Resin-glass and making sure no air bubbles remain underneath. Add more Resin-glass and continue arranging the pieces until the whole panel is finished.

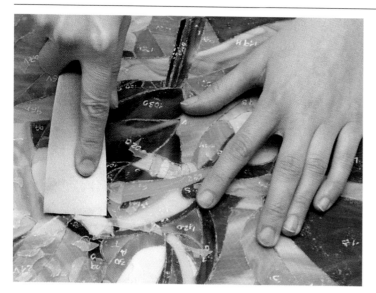

CLEANING THE DRIED RESIN

Wait until the Resin-glass solidifies and takes on a hard, rather rubbery consistency. Then, with a steel spatula, eliminate it from the entire panel surface, glass laths included. As drying time depends on the room temperature, it is best to pour on the Resin-glass in the morning so that you have the whole day to check to see if it solidifies. Do not let the Resin-glass over dry, otherwise it vitrifies and becomes practically impossible to remove it from the glass surface.

WAXING

Remove the masking tape covering the rear panel and clean off any Resin-glass that might have seeped in. Pour a small amount of glass wax onto a clean cotton cloth and pass it over the front and back of the panel. Leave to dry and then rub with a clean cloth.

The sun and clouds of this panel are of opalescent glass, while the sky is in light and dark blue cathedral glass. To highlight the plastic effect, the clouds are decorated with a slight dab of light blue while the stars are in gold. The eyes and the stars on the cheeks are in glass fusion.

MOCK STAINED GLASS

When making mock stained glass it is best to use cathedral glass. Thanks to its non-rigid structure, cathedral glass balances the light and makes it bright and vibrant. Soft shades are best because they delicately highlight the composition and permit the light to filter through: light yellow, aqua green, and old rose. Strong, deep colors create a gloomy atmosphere. It must be remembered that colored panels placed in window vanes filter the light and transmit the same tone of color to the inside. Therefore if a warm environment is desired, shades of pink, orange, or yellow must be chosen. Opalescent or colorescent glass (partly opaque) may also be used when you would like to reduce the light, prevent viewing from outside, or block uninteresting landscapes. Absolutely avoid colorless transparent glass (glass for window panes) which, although is easily available and cheap, shows the slightest errors in work and color imperfections. Where the pattern must be visible on both sides of the panel, apply the lead came on the rear as well.

SOME TECHNICAL TIPS

— Use glass of at least 1/8", otherwise it could break when the lead came is applied.
— Always work the glass on the smoothest side.
— Position the panel with the color turned inwards.
— Use only materials and tools specifically designed for this craft.
— Give great attention to cleanliness, particularly when applying lead came and the color paints.
— Do not wear clothes that shed lint.

MORE EQUIPMENT

BURNISHING ROD
Used to burnish lead in the joints and curves, and to straighten out bends and wrinkles.

BURNISHING ROLLER
This has a barrel-like wheel in hard rubber and is used to press the lead came onto the glass.

LEAD CAME KNIFE
Its stiff but sharp blade is used to cut the lead came along the joints, or to detach it when wrongly placed. The strong handle gives a comfortable, safe grip.

SOLDERING IRON
This special iron can melt solder but does not affect the adhesive lead came. The tip is long-life guaranteed for offering better resistance to the corrosive actions of the chemical agents used for soldering. It is best to clean the tip with sal ammoniac while the iron is still hot.

SOLDERING IRON STAND
This has been designed to avoid accidental burning.

FLUX BRUSH
Brushes for flux must have hard bristles in order for the liquid to penetrate into the channels of the lead came. They are specially made not to corrode.

FINE–TIPPED GLASS DROPPERS
Some decorations require the color paints to be spread by a dropper. Traditionally brushes were used, but this method guarantees a deeper color and the complete absence of any trace of brushwork, so as to simulate the uniform coloring of cathedral glass.

WOODEN SKEWER
These are used to carry the color paints to the end of the lead came.

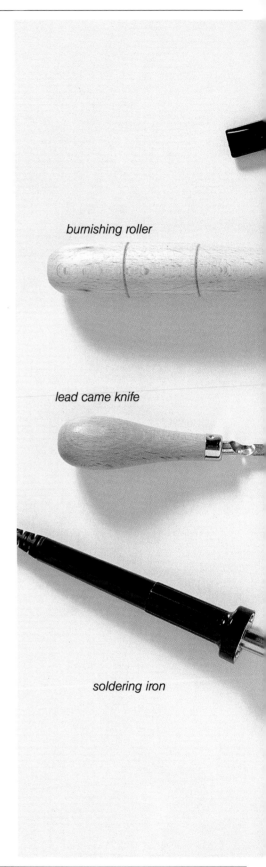

burnishing roller

lead came knife

soldering iron

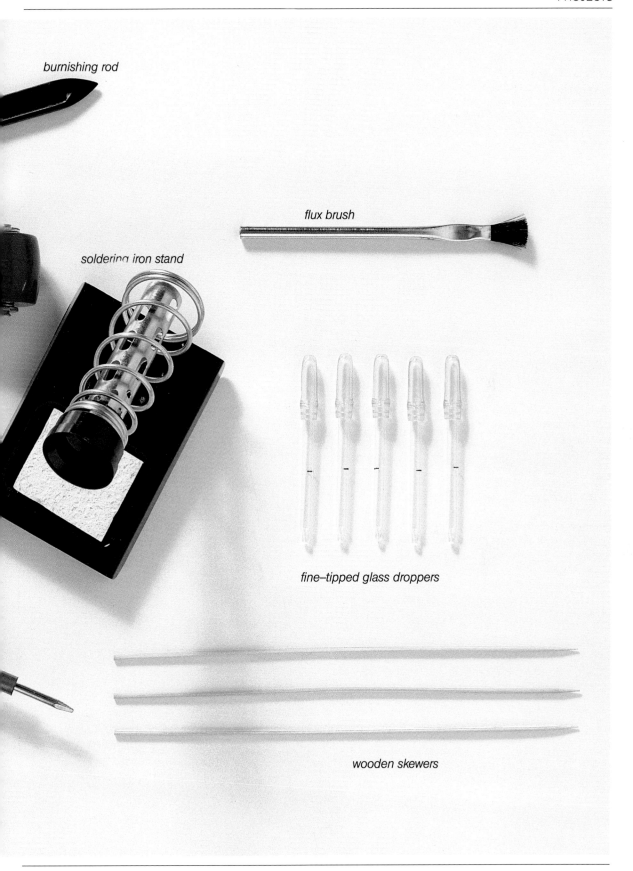

burnishing rod

flux brush

soldering iron stand

fine–tipped glass droppers

wooden skewers

REQUIRED MATERIAL

ADHESIVE LEAD CAME
A thin strip of paper protects the adhesive rear part of the lead came, which is removed when the came is applied to the glass. The came is very pliable and can follow meandering seams and tiny edge details. U-shaped came is available in two widths: 3/32" and 3/16", both in 6 ft. coils.

SOLDER
This comes in drawn rods. The solder must be top quality (without recycled mixtures) to avoid impurities surfacing later and oxidizing the soldered surface.

FLUX
This liquid, applied with a brush over the lead came, eliminates oxidation and allows the melted solder to adhere perfectly to the lead came.

BLACK PATINA
Natural came has the classical color of lead. By applying patina, a chemical reaction takes place which changes the coloring of the lead came and makes the tin and the lead colors uniform.

LEAD–CLEANING LIQUID
When rubbed on the natural or patina covered soldered seams, it makes them shine and protects them from oxidation and dampness.

SOLVENT COLORED PAINTS FOR GLASS
Various brands are offered in paint and stained glass shops, but we advise the use of the "Vetro Color" transparent colors for glass. They are the best for this type of work. There are 16 shades of color in this series which all can be mixed together. The deep, strong colors resist the light but, it must be noted that this resistance is proportionate to the thickness and to the degree of dilution of the applied colors. "Vetro Color" is easy to put on and results in decorations of notable transparency and homogeneity. Make sure to properly clean the support before use. This range comes with a thinner and a colorless varnish.

MOCK LEAD
This is an alternative to adhesive lead that gives added detail to the pattern. To obtain an even thickness it is best to evenly squeeze the tube, keeping the beak leaning on the support at a 45° angle. After 48 hours the empty spaces can be filled with the glass paints.

solder

black pa[tina]

flux

colored paints
for glass

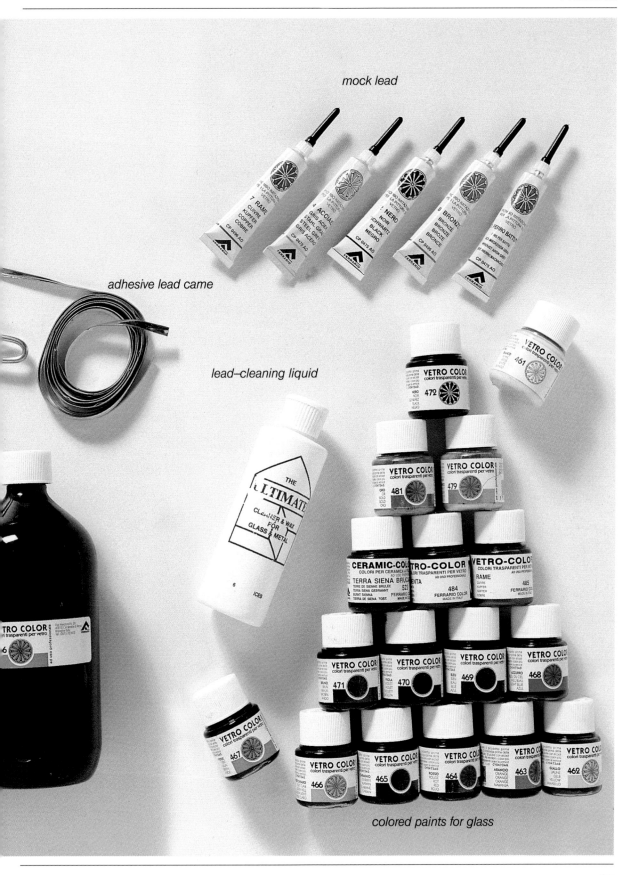

mock lead

adhesive lead came

lead–cleaning liquid

colored paints for glass

MAKING THE PANEL

REPRODUCING THE PATTERN ON GLASS

Lay the cathedral glass with the smoothest part facing upwards. Carefully clean it with a mixture of water and ammonia (80% - 20%), or a cleaning compound. Place the pattern at the rear of the glass sheet and secure it at the corners with adhesive tape to prevent it moving during work. Reproduce the pattern as faithfully and precisely as possible with a fine-tipped, silver colored felt pen for glass. When the tracing has been transferred it is ready for leading. If transparent glass has not been used, the pattern can be reproduced with tracing paper.

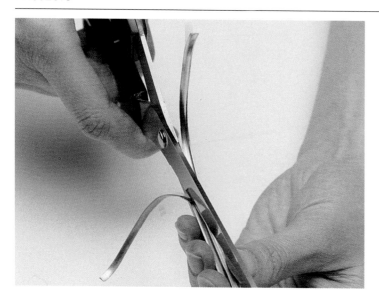

DIVIDING THE LEAD CAME

From the main coil cut a few segments of lead came measuring 20-25" (3/32" lead came is made double tracked). Then cut it lengthwise with ordinary scissors. Cut slowly and carefully to avoid snipping the borders.

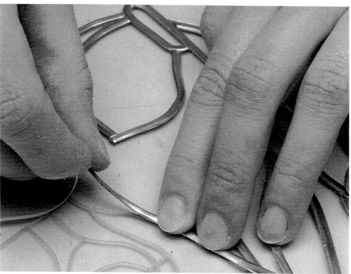

LAYING THE LEAD CAME

If the pattern is going to have a frame, it is best to begin from it and allow for wider came (5/32") than that used for the pattern (3/16"). Having decided the starting point, secure the end of the came to it. Slowly lay the lead came along. Make it adhere to the glass from left to right. When applying, take off the adhesive tape from the rear of the sheet. The glass must be cleaned often to remove the greasy marks left by your hands.

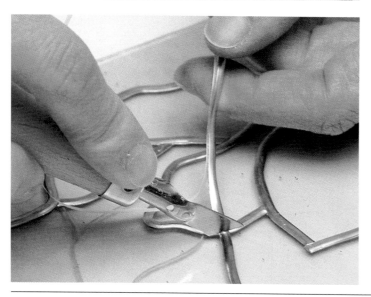

OVERLAPPING AND CUTTING THE LEAD CAME

When finishing, overlap the lead came 1/8". With the cutter firmly gripped, press and cut along the intersections. The joining of the lead came must be very precise, otherwise, the color could seep into the adjoining shape and mix with the other colors. If the lead came comes out short by mistake, it can be detached, stretched (lengthened), and replaced.

BURNISHING THE LEAD CAME

To be sure that the came adheres to the glass surface and to avoid from detaching, the burnisher must be passed back and forth many times along the whole lead seam. Though very soft, the came often shows up wrinkled or bent and it must then be modeled with the help of a wooden skewer to give it the required form.

PUTTYING THE LEAD CAME JOINTS

The joints must always be puttied before applying the colors, otherwise, the heat from the soldering iron will damage them. To carry out this operation, brush the junctures with some flux and then dab a small amount of solder. The solder must be spread evenly until the junction lines of the lead came are completely covered. As an alternative to only puttying the junctions, the whole came surface could be puttied. A panel made this way looks exactly like those prepared by the Tiffany technique.

APPLYING BLACK PATINA TO LEAD CAME

Before applying the patina, thoroughly clean with a solution of water and ammonia, or a cleaning compound, and then dry. Dip a cotton cloth in the patina liquid and rub the lead came repeatedly until a layer of black appears. Do not let more than a few hours pass between puttying and applying the patina. The lead came and the joints could oxidize and prevent the patina from taking effect. Copper patina should be used only on fully puttied lead came. It reacts to solder but not to lead.

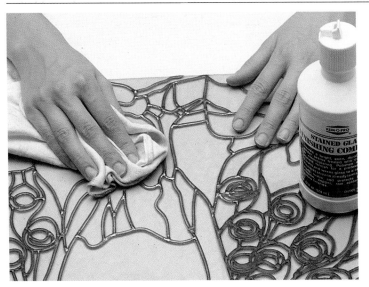

CLEANING AND POLISHING LEAD CAME

Once again dip a cloth in a solution of water and ammonia and clean your work, eliminating any excess patina, and then carefully dry. Pour a few drops of polishing cream on a clean cotton cloth and pass over the seams and the lead came. With another clean cloth, rub the seams and the glass until they shine. Do not leave traces of dust on the surface, as it could damage the color application.

COLORING THE PANEL

For a color to turn out flat, even, and glazed, it must be spread lavishly. Use a dropper, which makes it easier and quicker to paint wider areas than with a brush. Fill the dropper with the appropriate color and deposit it in the outlined areas by the lead came. Use the beak to help spread it.

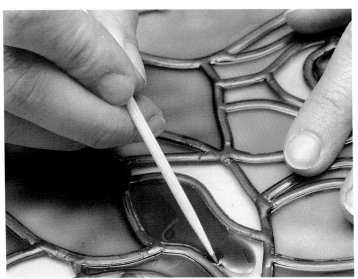

FINISHING THE COLORING

Be careful not to touch the lead came with the dropper, as it could stain. Use, instead, the wooden skewer to move the color to the lead came boundaries. Leave the panel to dry for a few days in a room without dust. Lay it horizontally, so the colors do not drip or mix.

ETCHED GLASS

A drawing made in 1897, by Muchà, *Salomè*, inspired our idea for this panel. The pattern has been subdivided into three complementary levels. Etching is carried out on three 1/8" glass pieces, which are then overlapped. This operation on various levels produces the three-dimensional effect. When dealing with complex projects, the initial stages are extremely important. With regards to preparing the designs, you must be very precise and make sure that the pieces match perfectly when overlapped. The pattern shown here could also be executed on one sheet, in which case you would use the whole pattern in its complete form.
It is also possible to work on a mirror. To obtain the tri-dimensional effect, there must be a transparent sheet of glass placed behind. The mirror surface and both sides of the transparent glass can then be etched.

SOME TECHNICAL TIPS

— Remember that motifs cut on the glass will be permanent.
— Carefully protect those parts of the glass that are not to be etched with adhesive plastic.
— To resist the impact of the various procedures, the thickness of the glass must be in proportion to the size of the panel.
— Sandblasting requires the same design preparation procedure as used for etching. Afterwards, it is necessary to resort to a specialized workshop for sandblasting with a compressor.
— Special adhesive templates with subjects for incision are available on the market. When attached to the glass with a spatula, they are ready to be etched.

MORE EQUIPMENT

SCALPEL WITH SPARE BLADES
This cuts the transparent adhesive plastic.

SMALL BRUSH
This is used to spread the etching cream.

METAL SPATULA WITH WOODEN HANDLE
This is also used for spreading and removing the etching cream.

LATEX GLOVES
They protect your skin.

SPONGE
This is used for cleaning the surface after using etching cream.

BURNISHING ROLLER
Use this to burnish the plastic to the glass.

REQUIRED MATERIAL

ADHESIVE TRANSPARENT PLASTIC FOR ETCHING
Make sure to purchase the proper type for this particular work.

ETCHING CREAM
This patented product scrapes off after being applied onto the glass.

FELT PEN
Use this to reproduce the tracing onto the plastic.

scalpel with spare blades

small brush

metal spatula with wooden handle

latex gloves

felt pen

adhesive transparent
plastic for etching

sponge

Armour Etch
Glass Etching Cream

etching cream

burnishing roller

MAKING THE PANEL

PREPARING THE POSITIVE/NEGATIVE PATTERN

Prepare a pattern for each of the three surfaces to be etched. The composition must be outlined without half-shades and with clean, precise strokes. The designs must be made on drawing paper so that they can be superimposed. Check to make sure that they match.

first level

second level

third level

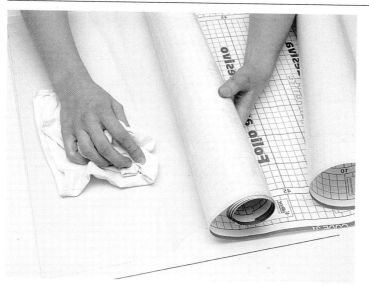

SECURING THE PLASTIC TO THE GLASS

Cut three panels of the same size and grind the borders to avoid cutting yourself. Thoroughly clean all of them. Place the plastic over the whole surface of the glass leaving no part uncovered. Lift a corner of the protecting paper and slowly make the plastic adhere with the help of a cloth. Make absolutely sure that no air bubbles remain between the plastic and the glass. If this occurs, raise the film once more and reposition it.

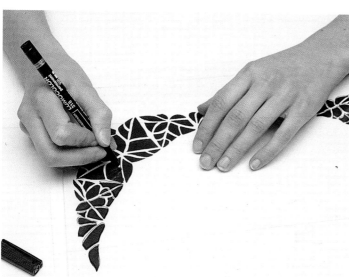

TRACING THE PATTERN ON THE PLASTIC

Secure the pattern to the rear of the glass with adhesive tape. Reproduce the traced design on the plastic with a permanent felt pen for glass. To reproduce the pattern, if using non-transparent glass, proceed as follows: place the pattern on the plastic (previously made to adhere to the glass), insert a sheet of carbon paper, and then trace the design.

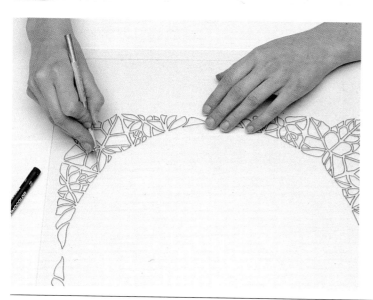

ETCHING THE PLASTIC

With a scalpel, score the border of the area to be etched in precise, fluid motions. It is important that the corners be cut very accurately to prevent the film from tearing when it is being removed.

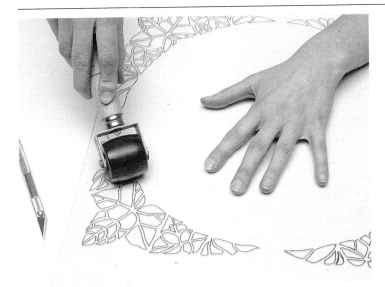

PASSING THE BURNISHING ROLLER

Pass the roller many times over the incisions made so that the plastic adheres to the glass.

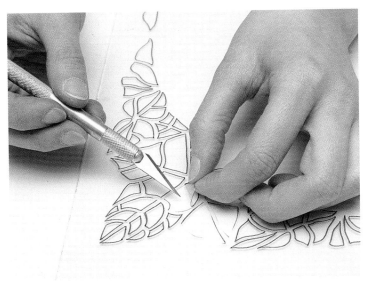

REMOVING THE PLASTIC IN THE AREAS TO BE ETCHED

When the incision of the whole design has been completed, remove the plastic with a scalpel from the areas to be etched. These will define the subject of the composition. As it is very easy to confuse the plastic areas to be removed, it is best to always keep the original drawing on hand.

APPLYING THE ETCHING CREAM

When carrying out this operation always use gloves and ventilate the room you are working in. With the appropriate brush apply a generous layer of etching cream over the uncovered areas of the glass. Spread it as evenly as possible leaving no part uncovered and being careful to leave no traces of brushstrokes. To etch wider areas, as here, use a steel spatula with a very pliable blade.

REMOVING THE ETCHING CREAM

Let the cream work for about 5 minutes or as instructed by the manufacture. Remove any excess with the spatula and rinse quickly with a sponge and lots of cold water. Dry thoroughly with a cotton cloth. Lay the etched glass on a dark cloth and check that no areas are uncovered by the etching. Where it is necessary, give the finishing touches with the etching cream.

REMOVING THE ADHESIVE PLASTIC

Still keeping the etched glass lying on a surface, use the scalpel where necessary to remove any remaining plastic. The pattern will now stand out. Clean with a product for cleaning glass and polish with the appropriate wax.

Characterized by its simplicity, this pattern could be used for small windows, furniture doors, small tables, and mirrors.

GRISAILLE

This pane was made to be inserted into the leaded panel shown in the chapter dedicated to traditional stained glass. The shape of the glass supporting the grisaille decoration can, however, be changed and adapted to various needs. The glass used for the grisaille is transparent cathedral glass. A grisaille of classical black tracing color was used for the edging. The nuances were made with dark brown grisaille. We thought it better not to burden the composition with too much color so as to let the design and chiaroscuro stand out. We also gave just a touch of golden yellow to the hair and light blue to the wings. (Detail from the *Birth of Venus* by Alexandre Cabanel)

SOME TECHNICAL TIPS

— Remember that grisaille, when baked, becomes a tone lighter.
— It is important to learn to use the correct quantity of gum Arabic to the grisaille. If the amount is too much, it cannot be removed to obtain shading.
— Bake the glass stretched out on the shelf of the furnace, and take it out only when cold. Many types of glass change their color if subjected to the grisaille baking temperature, therefore, check with a sample of the chosen glass before proceeding with your work.
— Some glass craftsmen use vinegar instead of water when preparing grisaille for edging. This procedure renders incompatible edging and half-shading (which should only be prepared with water). The edging, even if not previously baked, is not cancelled by the application of the half-shading. This procedure is rather complex and it is advisable to try it out on some samples before starting the definitive project.

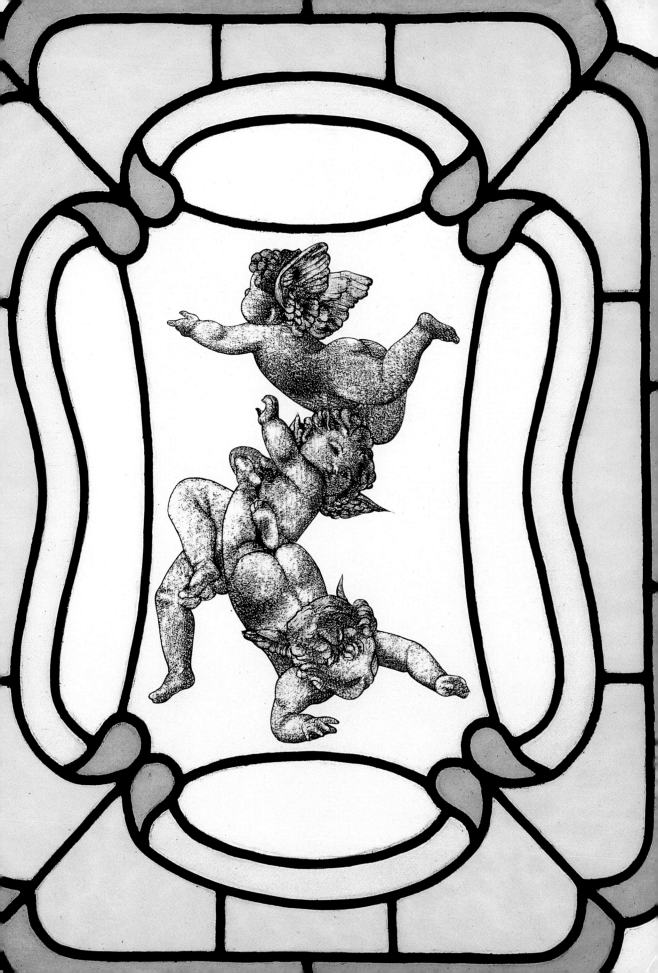

MORE EQUIPMENT

EDGING BRUSH
This has long, soft, and pliable bristles able to absorb a lot of color.
It is used with grisaille to outline the pattern (edging).

FLAT PAINT BRUSH FOR GLAZING
This must be at least 1/8" wide and have very soft, absorbent
bristles. It is used to spread the glazing and create shading.

DUSTING BRUSHES
These have short, rigid bristles and are used to remove the color
previously spread with the flat paintbrush.

SPATULA FOR POWDER COLORS
This is used for mixing and dissolving the colors.

FINE-TIPPED BRUSHES
These are used to spread the baked colors. They have a fine tip
and soft hairs.

ARM REST
This is essential to avoid accidentally touching the colors applied to
the glass.

GLASS PALETTE
This is used as a surface on which to mix colors.

BAKING FURNACE
This is a furnace for glass made of high-density ceramic fiber, which
is heated from above. It has a shell shaped opening and automatic
electric panel.

PEN
The grisaille can be applied with a pen on the thinnest stretches of
the pattern.

REQUIRED MATERIAL

GRISAILLES - 1,200°F
In shades of black, chestnut, brown, gray-green, and pale red, the
grisailles are mixed with water and gum arabic and then baked in
the furnace at about 1,200°F.

GUM ARABIC
This is used to make the color, mixed with water, adhere to the
glass. We advise the use of powdered gum arabic.

BAKING COLORS -1,020°F
These are in powder form and can be mixed into a paste with water
and a hydro-soluble medium. They bake at about 1,020°F during a
further baking after that of the grisaille.

HYDRO-SOLUBLE MEDIUM
This is a product which, when properly mixed with powered colors,
makes them fluid and ready to be spread in a soft, shaded manner.
It can be mixed with water to soften the coloring.

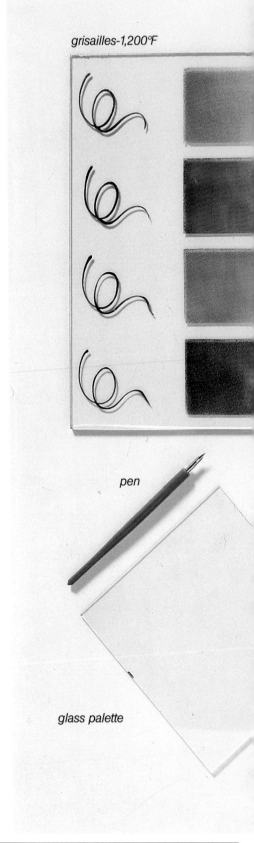

grisailles-1,200°F

pen

glass palette

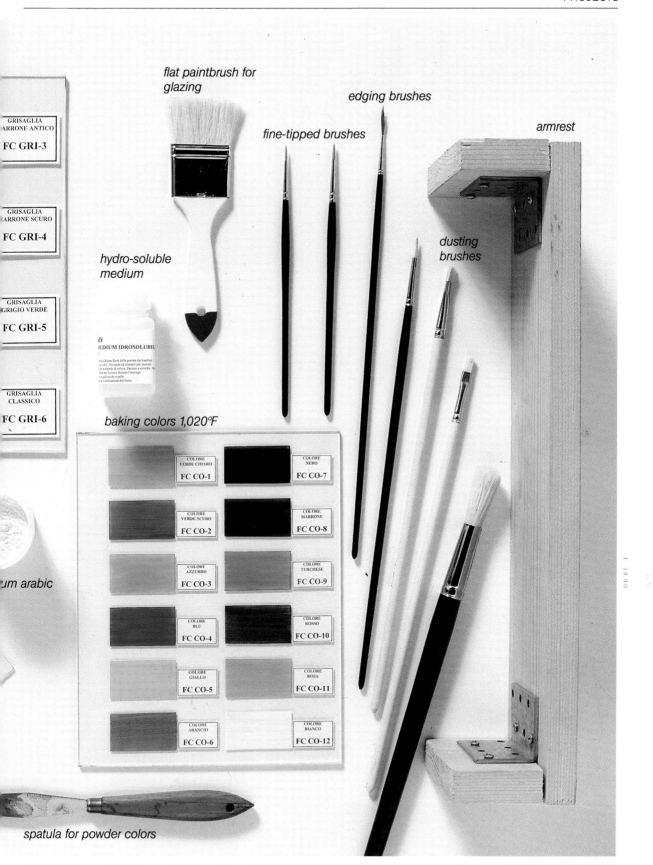

GRISAGLIA
ARRONE ANTICO
FC GRI-3

GRISAGLIA
ARRONE SCURO
FC GRI-4

GRISAGLIA
GRIGIO VERDE
FC GRI-5

GRISAGLIA
CLASSICO
FC GRI-6

flat paintbrush for glazing

edging brushes

fine-tipped brushes

armrest

dusting brushes

hydro-soluble medium

ft
EDIUM IDROSOLUBIL

baking colors 1,020°F

COLORE VERDE CHIARO **FC CO-1**	COLORE NERO **FC CO-7**
COLORE VERDE SCURO **FC CO-2**	COLORE MARRONE **FC CO-8**
COLORE AZZURRO **FC CO-3**	COLORE TURCHESE **FC CO-9**
COLORE BLU **FC CO-4**	COLORE ROSSO **FC CO-10**
COLORE GIALLO **FC CO-5**	COLORE ROSA **FC CO-11**
COLORE ARANCIO **FC CO-6**	COLORE BIANCO **FC CO-12**

um arabic

spatula for powder colors

Design with Chiaroscuros

MAKING THE PANEL

PREPARING THE PATTERN WITH CHIAROSCURO TRACING

Prepare the pattern to the scale of 1:1. It must be in black and white to highlight the chiaroscuro.

PREPARING THE PATTERN WITH DESIGN TRACING

Place a sheet of drawing paper on the prepared pattern and, with fine, clear strokes, highlight only the lines of the subject such as the face, clothes, and decorative lines. This design will serve as a guide for the edging.

Outlined design

Finished design on glass

PREPARING THE GRISAILLE

Pour a little grisaille on the palette and add a dab of gum Arabic. Then add a few drops of water and mix. Knead the formed paste with the spatula.

AMALGAMATING THE POWDERS

Continue working the paste with the spatula and adding water until no powder grains remain. The color obtained should have the consistency of Indian ink.
To keep the color consistent when edging the pattern, keep adding water and amalgamate it with the paste using the spatula.

EDGING THE DESIGN

Clean the panel to remove any greasy stains. Use a solution of water (80%) and ammonia (20%), or a cleaning compound. Place the glass on the pattern bearing the traced design and secure it with adhesive tape. Dip the brush in the color trying to absorb as much as possible. Lean on the armrest and brush stroke holding the brush almost vertically. Let the brush pass along slowly. With one motion, try to obtain a full, flowing stroke. Dip in the color once more and make the next stroke beginning exactly from where the last one ended. If you make a mistake, remove the color with a clean cloth.

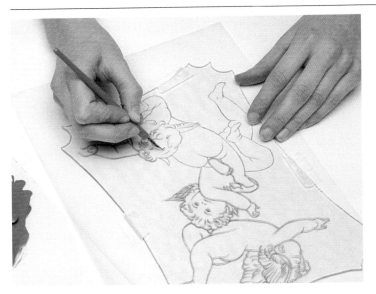

EDGING WITH A PEN

For the thinnest lines such as the hair or where greater detail is required, grisaille can be applied with a pen. Try this out on a sample before starting your real work.

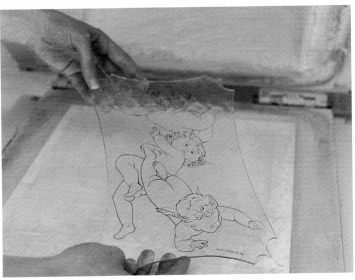

BAKING

Lay the glass on the furnace shelf and set the temperature at 1,200°F. When this has been reached, turn off and leave to cool. Do not put the glass to bake in a vertical or inclined position, as it tends to deform at this temperature.

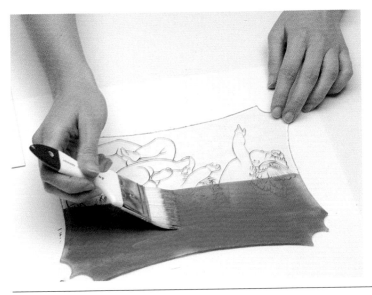

GLAZING THE GRISAILLE

Mix the grisailles, adding more water to obtain greater color transparency. With wide motions of the paintbrush, apply the paste over the whole glass surface. Movement must be from top to bottom and then from left to right so you create an even layer. Work quickly making sure to finish before the color dries.

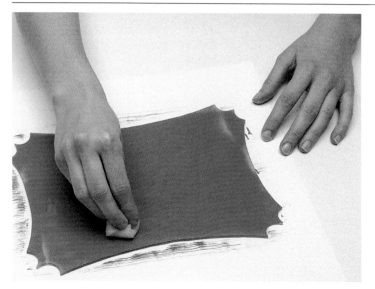

SPONGING THE GRISAILLE

It is possible to give a decorative texture to the glazing by tapping its surface when still wet with a sponge or brush.

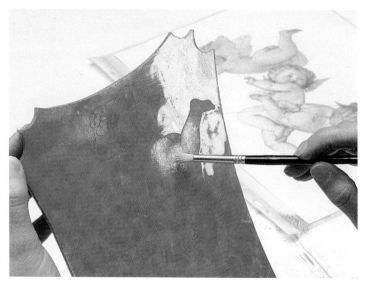

BRUSHING THE GRISAILLE

Wait until the glazing is completely dry (after about 10-15 minutes). Then with the brushes for shading, remove the color from the areas where light will pass to create a shady effect. Also do this for the pattern with the chiaroscuro tracing.

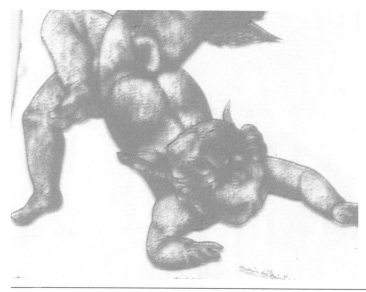

BRUSHING THE GRISAILLE (WORK FINISHED)

Creating half-shading is a long and difficult step. It is better to proceed slowly because mistakes at this stage might mean having to redo the glazing. Bake the glass once more in the furnace at a temperature of 1,200°F.

PREPARING THE COLOR

As already mentioned, the traditional grisaille technique involves only edging and half-shading, while color is given by the glass itself. If the project allows, however, it is possible to give color to the design. Put a little powder color on the palette and add a few drops of hydro-soluble medium and water. Work with the spatula until the color has completely dissolved.

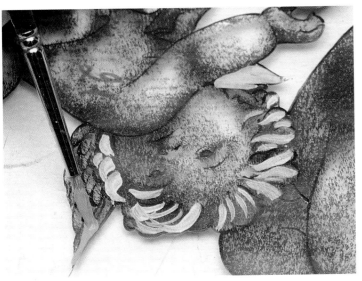

COLORING DETAILS

Paint the areas involved with a brush, spreading the color on the side where the grisaille was laid, or on the rear.

BAKING AND INSERTION OF THE LEADED GLASS

Bake the glass once more, this time at about 1,020°F. It is impossible to bake grisaille just once because the colors would burn and become opaque, losing their brilliancy. Let the glass cool and take it out of the furnace. At this point you may insert it in the composition (see the chapter on working with traditional stained glass).

DESIGNS

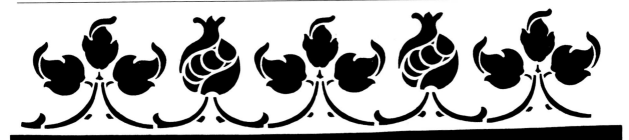

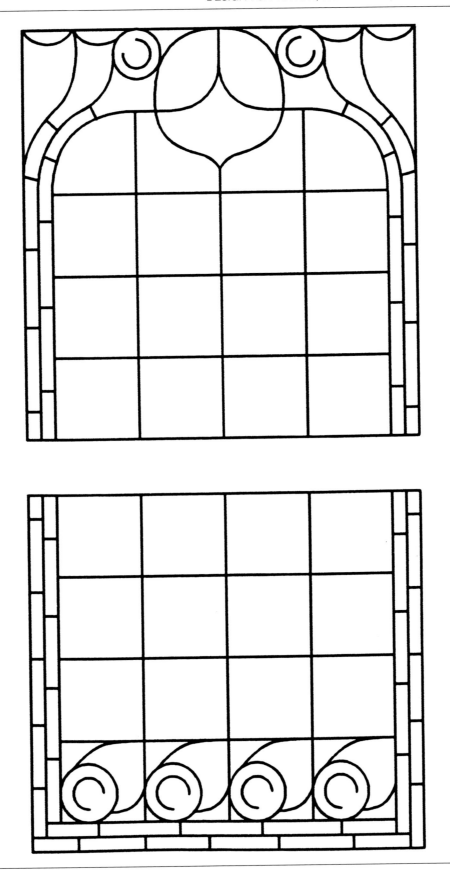

INDEX